The Tarot Journey in Colour

The Tarot Journey in Colour

Your Complete Guide to Tarot Mastery

Sasha Fenton

Zambezi Publishing Ltd

First published in 2024 in the UK by Zambezi Publishing Ltd
Plymouth, Devon PL2 2YJ
Tel: +44 (0)1752 367 300
zambezipub@gmail.com   www.zampub.com

Text copyright ©2024 Sasha Fenton
Sasha Fenton has asserted the moral right to be identified
as the author of this work.

British Library Cataloguing in Publication Data:
A catalogue record for this book is available from the British Library

ISBN(13) 978-1-915176-01-1

Illustrations copyright © 2024 Jan Budkowski
Advisory note: all images apart from author photo
have been created with the help of AI resources.
All text has been written without using AI.

Typesetting by Zambezi Publishing Ltd, Plymouth

All rights reserved. No part of this publication may be reproduced, stored in a retrieval system, or transmitted in any form or by any means, electronic, mechanical, photocopying, recording or otherwise, whether currently existing or yet to be developed, without the prior written permission of the publisher. This book is sold subject to the condition that it shall not, by way of trade or otherwise, be lent, resold, hired out or otherwise circulated without the publisher's prior written consent, in any form of binding, cover or format other than that in which it is originally published, and without a similar condition being imposed on the subsequent purchaser.

Disclaimer:- This book is intended to provide general information regarding the subject matter, and to entertain. The contents are not exhaustive and no warranty is given as to accuracy of content. The book is sold on the understanding that neither the publisher nor the author are thereby engaged in rendering professional services, in respect of the subject matter or any other field. If expert guidance is required, the services of a qualified professional should be sought.

Readers are urged to access a range of other material on the book's subject matter, and to tailor the information to their individual needs. Neither the author nor the publisher shall have any responsibility to any person or entity regarding any loss or damage caused or alleged to be caused, directly or indirectly, by the use or misuse of information contained in this book. If you do not wish to be bound by the above, you may return this book in original condition to the publisher, with its receipt, for a refund of the purchase price.

About the Author

Sasha Fenton has transformed her childhood fascination with Palmistry and Astrology into a successful career, expanding her expertise to include Tarot and the development of her psychic abilities. Since 1973, she has worked as a professional consultant, gradually reducing her involvement as her writing career took off.

To date, Sasha has authored an impressive total of 142 books, mostly published by various mainstream publishers worldwide.

In addition to her literary accomplishments, Sasha has also made significant contributions to magazines and newspapers. She wrote the stars page for Woman's Own Magazine for six years, and prior to that, she contributed to the Sunday People's Magazine for a couple of years. Sasha's syndicated column appeared in numerous local papers, and she has written about 3,000 articles and columns for publications of all kinds, including nearly every national newspaper in the UK.

Sasha's expertise has also been showcased on television and radio. She has made appearances on various BBC and independent radio stations, both as a guest and with her own regular segments. Sasha has also hosted her own television shows, primarily focusing on astrology but occasionally exploring other aspects of divination.

Sasha's public engagement extends to numerous festivals in the UK and overseas, where she has delivered talks and workshops. Notable events include the prominent festivals in London, Melbourne, and Sydney.

Furthermore, Sasha has held key positions within various organisations. She served as President of the British Astrological and Psychic Society (BAPS) on two occasions and chaired the Advisory Panel on Astrological Education (APAE). Additionally, she was a member of the Executive Council of the Writers' Guild of Great Britain, and she served on the Committee of the Federation of Small Businesses. Sasha also twice played a pivotal role in organising Plymouth Small Business Saturday events. Currently, she holds the position of Joint Managing Director in MBS Professionals Ltd, Stellium Ltd, and Zambezi Publishing Ltd.

Zambezi Publishing Ltd, which Sasha and her husband, Jan Budkowski, established in November 1996, has been instrumental in producing hundreds of books, primarily in the mind, body, and spirit genre. Many of these publications have gone on to become co-editions and series with prominent publishers in the UK and overseas.

Other Books by Sasha Fenton

The Tudorland Series
Sophie's Inheritance
Lucy's Dilemma
Emily's Mistake

Astrology
Astrology East and West
Astrology for Living
Astrology for Wimps
Astrology in Focus: How to Find Your Rising Sign
How to Read Your Star Signs
In Focus: Astrology
Moon Signs
Astrological Cycles in Focus
Rising Signs
Sasha Benton's Moon Signs
Sasha Fenton's Planets
Sasha Fenton's Reading the Future
Sasha Fenton's Rising Signs
Sun Signs
The Hidden Zodiac
The Moon in Focus
Understanding Astrology
Understanding the Astrological Vertex
Astrology in Focus: Decans and Dwaads
Ten years of contribution to Llewellyn's Sun Sign Book
The BIG Astrology Guide: Volume One
The BIG Astrology Guide: Volume Two

With the Late Jonathan Dee
Sun Signs Made Simple
The Moon Sign Kit
Star*Date*Oracle
Astro-guides – from 1995 to 2000 (*72 full sized books*)
Your Millennium Forecasts
Forecasts 2001
Forecasts 2002

Astro-Numerology
Astro-Numerology: A Small Handbook

Palmistry
Hand Reading
In Focus: Palmistry
Learning Palmistry
Living Palmistry

Modern Palmistry
Simply Palmistry
The Book of Palmistry
The Living Hand

Tarot
Elementary Tarot
Fortune-Telling by Tarot Cards
How to Find Love in the Tarot (*ebook only*)
Super Tarot
Tarot in Action!
Tarot Masters (*contribution*)
The Tarot

Chinese
Chinese Divinations
Elementary I Ching
Feng Shui for the Home
The Flying Stars
In Focus: Chinese Astrology

Psychic, Spiritual, Fortune Telling
Body Reading
Dream Meanings
Dreams (*with Jan Budkowski*)
Fortune-Teller's Handbook
Fortune-Teller's Workbook
Fortune-Telling by Tea Leaves
How to Be Psychic
In Focus: Chakras
In Focus: Numerology
Simply Chakras
Spells
Spells in Focus
Tea Cup Reading
The Aquarian Book of Fortune Telling

Health
Diabetes: An Everyday Guide

Business
Prophecy for Profit (*with Jan Budkowski*)
The Money Book (*with Jan Budkowski*)
Self-Publishing with Stellium

Contents

Introduction: Who Is This Book For? 3
1: About the Tarot 6
2: Make Your Tarot Cards Work For You 18
3: Major Arcana 25
4: The Minor Arcana 70
5: The Suit of Wands 73
6: The Suit Of Cups 89
7: The Suit Of Pentacles 105
8: The Suit Of Swords 121
9: Some Simple Tarot Spreads 136
10: Complex Spreads 148
11: How To Link Cards Together To Tell A Story 155
12: Colour And The Tarot 162
13: Quick Clues To The Meanings Of The Cards 170
14: Tarot And Numbers 180
15: Tarot And The Decans 184
16: A Couple Of Readings In Action 191
17: Spell Casting 198
18: Journalling 202
19: Tarot As A Profession 207
20: Your First Fee Paying Client 210
Conclusion 213
Index 214

The Tarot Journey in Colour

Introduction: Who Is This Book For?

This book is for anyone interested in reading Tarot cards, whether they are beginners or professionals. It guides beginners who struggle with linking the cards to create a coherent story and offers additional ideas for more experienced readers.

Some individuals have a strong right brain that connects with images, colours, shapes, and the concepts they convey. These individuals prefer to read the cards based on the pictures rather than memorising the meanings. This book also provides advice for these readers. However, for those who like to look up card meanings, the book starts with conventional interpretations in the chapters dedicated to card meanings. It also includes any supplementary or alternative meanings that may apply. Additionally, it offers insights on interpreting cards that may initially seem confusing.

***

Throughout this book, the capital "T" is used for Tarot. The terms "reader" or "consultant" refer to the person giving the reading, while the recipient is referred to as the "questioner" or "client."

***

My Introduction to the Tarot

There used to be a belief that buying your own Tarot cards was unlucky and that they should be given to you as a gift. While this is nothing more than a myth, many people do receive their first deck as a gift and then explore different decks until they find one that resonates with them. It is important to use cards that speak to you. With that in mind, here is the story of my first Tarot deck.

In the autumn of 1975, my mother bought me a gift she had come across in a shop. It was a box containing a Tarot card deck, a small book, and a poster illustrating the Celtic Cross layout.

The Tarot Journey in Colour

At that time, I was working as a filing clerk for a recruitment agency, spending my days pulling out files for the recruiters and putting the files back when they had finished with them. I also gave occasional palmistry and astrology readings at home during weekends, but the New Age era was taking off at the time and my clients were telling me that I should learn the Tarot.

I was wondering how to go about this when my mother bought me a Tarot gift set that she had seen in a shop. The kit contained a deck of cards, a poster showing the Celtic Cross layout and a small book of interpretations. The deck was the Swiss Tarot, in which only the Major Arcana is fully illustrated. The Minor Arcana is therefore more like a set of playing cards than a Tarot deck. The little book was filled with ancient warnings about death, destruction and misery. I couldn't make any headway with it, so I took it to work the next day and when lunch hour came around, my friend Kay joined me and we both tried to make sense of the cards.

There we were, with the cards spread out in front of us, when one of the senior managers walked in. To our astonishment, he walked over to my workbench, picked up all the cards, turned on his heel and walked to the door without saying a word. As he walked out of the room, he looked back over his shoulder and said, "Be in my office at one o'clock tomorrow."

We were terrified! In those days, many people considered Tarot to be "occult" and potentially dangerous., and some individuals were very apprehensive about it. Both Kay and I needed our jobs, and we were convinced that our future at the company was over. Nevertheless, we showed up at the senior manager's office the next day.

To our utter amazement, he was seated at the head of a boardroom table with the foldout poster in front of him. He divided the cards into two piles, one smaller than the other. Handing the smaller pile to Kay, he asked her to shuffle the cards, instructing her to return them once she felt they were sufficiently mixed. Using the poster, he laid out the Celtic Cross spread, using only the Major Arcana cards. He gave Kay a reading that accurately described what was happening in her life and even provided a remarkably accurate prediction for her future. He then did the same for me, with equally amazing results.

We later discovered that this very helpful manager had spent two years in Romania, where he had befriended the local Romany Gypsies. During his time there, they had taught him to read Tarot, albeit using only the twenty-two cards of the Major Arcana.

Introduction

I abandoned the kit my mother had bought me and treated myself to a Rider Waite deck. I also delved into my collection of Prediction magazines, which contained numerous insightful articles on the Tarot. While my main focus was on astrology and palmistry, I offered free Tarot readings to my clients for a few months before providing them with their "proper" astrology readings. This helped me establish connections between what I saw in the cards and the reality of their lives and futures. Not a single client declined the offer, and this experience helped me to gain knowledge and confidence. Over time, I began writing books and conducting Tarot workshops worldwide.

The Tarot Card Images

The deck of cards used in this book is also called "The Tarot Journey", specifically designed to complement this book.

A specially printed edition of these beautiful cards will be available fairly soon, probably by the end of July this year. It will be available on Amazon and other online bookshops, and directly from us at Zambezi Publishing Ltd. Email us at *zambezipub@gmail.com* for more details, pricing and delivery.

1: About the Tarot

There are an incredible number of views about the origins of the Tarot, and many experts are happy to give us their opinions – only for other experts to disagree. Some ancient books say that the Tarot came from India or Tibet, while others are certain that it grew out of the Kabbalah. These days, many are convinced that the Tarot is ancient Egyptian in origin, while others are equally confident that the cards began life in China. I have even read that it was invented by Tibetan monks living in Scotland! I believe the images originated in various places, and they eventually came together and made their way to Europe.

It is known that playing cards reached Europe during the 13th century. An early form of playing cards was the Mamluk deck, which had four suits: Sticks, Pentacles, Swords and Cups, with ten numerical cards and three court cards, making them recognisable prototypes for both playing cards and Tarot cards. The first known Tarot deck is the Visconti-Sforza Tarot, hand-painted in Milan during the 15th century. Fifteen cards were painted for the Duke of Milan, Filippo Maria Visconti and his son-in-law, Francesco Sforza, but the deck was known as Trionfi and it was used for game playing.

Early decks include the Sola-Busca, the Minchiati and the Boiardo-Viti Tarocchi. The Sola-Busca features Roman gods and mythical stories and is the first deck to have all the cards illustrated rather than simple pip designs on the numbered cards. The Jean Noblet cards were produced in Paris around 1650.

With the invention of the printing press, both playing card and Tarot decks became accessible to the masses, and both were used for games and gambling.

Cards started to be used for fortune telling around 1750, and we know this because a deck called the Tarocco Bolognese contained a book that listed interpretations for each card. However, an increase of interest in all things esoteric in 19th century France really moved the Tarot story forward, especially when Jean-Baptiste Alliette, alias Etteilla, popularised the Marseille Tarot, which is still around today.

At around the turn of the 20th century, the Hermetic Order of the Golden Dawn produced two decks, one of which was the Thoth deck by Aleister Crowley. Arthur Edward Waite designed the other, and it became the Rider Waite deck. Waite may have designed the deck, but the artist

1: About the Tarot

who drew the illustrations was Pamela Colman-Smith, and she fully illustrated each card, making them easy for everyone to understand. The Thoth Tarot by Aleister Crowley is beautiful but hard to understand because Lady Frieda Harris's illustrations encompass symbolism from the Kabbalah and astrology, so it only really makes sense to those who have a thorough knowledge of those forms of divination.

The New Age arrived in the UK in the 1970s, and it carried on throughout the 1980s, bringing a significant interest in Eastern ideas such as Buddhism and meditation. It also raised interest in divinations such as the Tarot, which had hitherto been condemned as "occult". This also coincided with advances in printing processes. Now, Tarot is so acceptable that thousands of decks and books are available, and there are millions of Tarot readers worldwide. Tarot is easy to learn and it is practical, which is why it is so popular.

What Do You Need From the Cards?

You may need advice on love and relationships, career and finance, family and home, health and welfare, self-knowledge, self-development or spiritual knowledge. You may want to find your spiritual purpose, which may be to help others, look after your family, be creative, travel the world, grow food or a million other things. A Tarot reading might help you focus on your future pathway.

Fate or Free Will?

The cards will often confirm what the questioner already had in mind to do, but when something unexpected shows up, fate may soon intervene in the questioner's life. The questioner can disregard fate and insist on using their free will, but whether this works or not is a moot point. I believe that most of the time, we do what we want, but once in a while, destiny takes a hand, and we have no choice but to go with the flow.

We See Shadows

A reader called Carina once told me that we see shadows rather than clear messages, and we have to interpret these as well as we can. Not every reading is as clear as daylight, and sometimes there is a slight misfire. For instance, a reader recently told a friend of mine that she would take in a dog that needed to be looked after. My friend knew she couldn't cope with a dog, and if someone asked her to do so, she would have to refuse. As it happened, her next-door neighbour took in a relative's dog for a while, so the reader got the dog right and the area right but not the person.

Nevertheless, everyone was happy with the outcome of this reading. This kind of slight misfire is nothing unusual.

Keep it Real

We need to take a responsible attitude to Tarot readings but also accept that there are limits to what we can do, regardless of what clients expect of us. We should tread a careful path between being honest and coming out with things that would frighten our questioners. For example, if you suspect a client has a health problem coming up, you could tell them that they may feel off-colour soon and that it would be worth going to a doctor to put their mind at rest, after which it falls to the client to take your advice or to ignore it.

Don't dramatise yourself or try to make yourself exciting. I remember one reader who went to great pains to make herself theatrical by coming out with things that were completely over the top and on some occasions, complete rubbish. So, she told one poor man that he would die of the bubonic plague, and not too far into the future!

Worse still, I have known men who offer Tarot readings to attract women's attention. I remember seeing one idiot who tried to hold the attention of a female bar worker in a busy pub by laying out a spread of cards for her on the counter while she was busy pulling pints, thereby trying to draw her attention away from the men who wanted her to pour their drinks.

Some readers won't give information about a third person. For instance, if a questioner is going through a divorce, they won't say anything about the other person in the equation. This is a tricky one to cope with, so I suggest that when you mention other people, you should be very careful about how you do so, especially if your client records the session. Never be openly critical of the other person other than to suggest they may be difficult at times.

Despite what your client wants to believe, you are not a doctor, lawyer, accountant, builder or any other kind of specialist, so all you can do is tell your clients what you see, be sympathetic to their plight and suggest they take appropriate advice from a qualified professional.

An Example

Here is a true story about a man who I will call Rodney. Rodney had made some really bad investments, which had gone even further down the drain when a recession came. Poor Rodney was in a real pickle, and he wanted me to tell him where to find great investments that would replace his lost fortune. I pointed out that I was in no position to give investment advice,

1: About the Tarot

but Rodney was certain that I had a trick or two up my sleeve and that I was holding out on him. I pointed out very politely that if I knew how to make a fortune from investments, I'd hardly be sitting in the back room of my small house earning money by doing readings!

The Impossible Dream

Some clients want to become rich, famous and successful, but lack training, talent or luck. Suppose you can't see a glittering future on the cards for your client. In that case, all you can do is suggest they find work in the area of their chosen field and hope that an opening might arise, like being a roady to a rock band, and hoping to join the band one day.

I guess the thing to fall back upon is the Hippocratic Oath that doctors swear to, which starts with words along the lines of: "First, do no harm."

Energising a New Deck

Take your cards out of their box and hold them in your hands while imagining white light and blessings beaming down on them. Ask the universe to give the cards the energy they need to heal and help those who consult them and those who use them. If you like using incense sticks, you can wave your cards around in the incense to clear them of harmful vibrations and imbue them with good ones. You might want to put a favourite crystal on top of the deck for a while to encourage the deck to work well and protect it.

If you feel someone has put an unwanted influence onto your cards, re-energise them as you would a new deck.

Looking After Your Cards

Your cards are an important tool, so keep them away from children, pets and curious friends. The Chinese believe that divination tools should be kept on a shelf higher than one's head so that they are closer to heaven than we are, so you might like to do that yourself.

Some people like to wrap their cards in a silk scarf and tuck them into a special bag, while others keep them in a pretty box. I keep my cards in boxes without wrapping them in silk, and whenever I am in an area with gift shops or New Age shops, I look around for fancy boxes for my Tarot decks. My late friend Jonathan Dee was more traditional, so he always wrapped his cards in silk and tucked them into a purple satin Tarot bag. It is a matter of personal choice.

Oddly enough, the idea of wrapping cards in silk stems from ancient Japan, and specifically from Japanese warriors. It is said that they wrapped their bodies in silk before a battle because silk has a very fine weave and is also very strong, so if they got shot by an arrow during a battle, the arrow would go into their bodies carrying the silk with it. This made it easier for the medics to extract the arrow and it prevented infection from entering the wound, hence the idea of silk being protective.

Shuffle the Cards
Shuffle new cards a lot before you start to use them, as this takes off some of the shine and makes the cards easier to use, while shuffling also stirs the cards so that you get a good mixture of cards in each reading. Another reason is that handling the cards puts your own aura and energy into them.

Other Cards
Oracle cards look lovely, and they can be fun to read but they aren't Tarot. Playing cards are similar to the Tarot but if you fancy learning to use them, you should treat yourself to a book on the subject.

Where to Read the Cards
You can read Tarot cards anywhere: on the dining room table, in the kitchen, or even on the floor. Use a pretty cloth to lay the cards on, keeping them clean and making the reading memorable.

Shuffling
Some people like to give the cards to the questioner to shuffle, and others want to shuffle themselves. If you shuffle the cards yourself, you must ask your questioner to say "stop" when they feel you have shuffled enough. If your questioner shuffles the cards, ask them to shuffle until they think they've done enough.

One benefit of asking the questioner to do the shuffling is that it allows you to see how they go about it, as this tells you a little about the client. For instance, some clients will quickly shuffle the cards and hand them back with an expectant look, while others shuffle for so long that you wonder if they will ever stop.

Once your questioner has done the shuffling, you can ask them to lay the cards down lengthwise in front of them, cut them into two or three piles, and then choose one of the piles for you to read. This isn't necessary, but it is a nice touch, as is asking them to use their left hand for this as it is nearer to the heart.

1: About the Tarot

Now, lay the cards down in your favourite spread and give yourself time to think about what the cards are saying. Before diving into the reading, try to pick up an overview of what's going on in the questioner's life. I will explore this kind of thing in depth later in this book.

A Significator
The idea of a significator is to find a card that represents the questioner and then lay a spread over the top of that card. If you want to use significators, please go ahead, but most people don't bother. It takes time to find one, and it removes a card from the deck, which may be a drawback.

Reversed Cards
A reversed card lies upside down in a spread. Many years ago, readers shuffled the cards in such a way that many of them would be reversed. They would give these cards separate meanings from the upright ones, but people don't bother with reversed cards these days.

The Tarot Journey in Colour

I think the idea of reversed cards came from playing card reading, which was far more popular than Tarot in days gone by. Playing cards were freely available and inexpensive, while Tarot cards were hard to find and costly. It made sense to double up the meanings of playing cards when you consider that there are only fifty-two cards in a deck plus the Joker, so giving each card two meanings made it easier for readers to develop a worthwhile story from them. The reader needed to mark the Court cards so they knew which way was upright and which was reversed.

A reversed card that turns up by accident in a spread will draw your attention, and you can judge the card in any way that you think fit. For instance, some readers consider a reversed card to represent something that has already happened, while others see it as something still in the future. Alternatively, the energy of a reversed card can be diluted; for instance, a good card may become less beneficial, while a difficult card suggests that a problem will be less bothersome than it might otherwise be.

I will give brief meanings for the reversed cards later in case you need some inspiration when one turns up in a reading.

Your Interpretation is the Right One
When teaching the Tarot, I always tell students that what they think a card means is the correct interpretation, even if it goes against the accepted meaning of the card, because a combination of intuition and something that bubbles up from the image on the card will often give you the correct answer. Readers can find themselves reading the same cards in different ways on different occasions. A classic example is the Queen of Swords, as this can represent a real battle-axe on the one hand but an intelligent and educated professional who will give the client good advice on the other.

If you are a visual, artistic and "right-brain" person, you will find the illustrations on your cards immensely helpful. For instance, I recently saw a man on the television giving someone a reading and pointing to the Four of Cups. He said, "There will soon be an opportunity that will come out of the blue." The standard meaning for the Four of Cups is that the questioner is ignoring the good things they have and yearning for something they think they are missing, but the card could easily indicate something nice coming out of the blue, so I have added this idea as an alternative meaning for this card.

1: About the Tarot

Similarly, I remember someone once telling me that whenever he saw the Devil card in a reading, it said to him that the person suffered from a skin ailment. He reasoned that the image on the card represented the burning sensation that can accompany a skin problem owing to the connection between the Devil and the fires of hell! The skin disease idea struck me as being sensible, so I have added it as a supplementary meaning in the interpretations chapter.

If you often link a particular card to something that is not the "standard" meaning, by all means, use your own interpretation.

Court Cards

Court cards can be difficult. Some Tarot readers talk about fair-haired women or dark-haired men coming into the questioner's life, while others use astrology and say that a Sagittarian lad or a Taurus woman is on the way into the client's life. Some people see the Wand and Sword cards as Yang and active, and the Cup and Coin cards as Yin and passive, which can be helpful.

If any of this helps, that's fine. Still, it may be easier to look at the character of the Court card and see how it affects the reading or how the person in the Court card is influenced by the conditions shown in the reading. For instance, a lovely, kind lady like the Queen of Cups would be an excellent omen for a man looking for love. On the other hand, she could be pleasant and helpful to someone who is trying to buy a house or someone who has to deal with an unhappy child.

Archetypes

An archetype might be an earth mother type, a whizz kid, a sober and solid working man, a reliable friend, a troublemaker and so on. You will develop your own ideas about types of people associated with certain cards as you go along, and you might want to note these down in your journal while you are getting used to the Tarot.

A word being bandied around in intellectual circles these days is trope. It means an archetype or a metaphor. In short, something that stands for something else, such as a description like "a person who is as useful as a chocolate teapot, "a motherly figure", and so on.

The Tarot Journey in Colour

The Arcanas
A Tarot deck is split into two Arcanas. Arcana means secret or hidden knowledge.

The Major Arcana
There are twenty-two Major Arcana cards, each with a powerful meaning that can show a significant event or turning point in the questioner's life.

The Minor Arcana
The Minor Arcana is the everyday feature of the Tarot because it talks about the things that happen to us daily. Having said that, Minor Arcana cards can also refer to some pretty significant events. The Minor Arcana comprises four suits, similar to those in a deck of playing cards. The suits can have various names, but in this book, I will use the standard names that all Tarot readers understand. These names are Wands, Cups, Pentacles and Swords, and. I often call the Coin cards Pentacles because most decks have a pentacle design on this suit.

Alternative names for the suits can be:
Wands: Rods, Batons, Staves or Sceptres.
Cups: Chalices or Cauldrons.
Pentacles: Pentacles or Discs.
Swords: I have only ever seen these called Swords.

The connection to playing cards works like this:
Wands: Clubs.
Cups: Hearts.
Pentacles: Diamonds.
Swords: Spades.

More About the Minor Arcana
Whatever people believe about the origins of the Tarot, somewhere along the line, it became linked to the medieval and renaissance courts of Europe; this becomes evident when one looks at the Court cards with their Kings, Queens, Knights and Pages. However, other decks might swap the Knights and Pages for Princes and Princesses. The Court cards show some similarity to both playing cards and chess pieces.

1: About the Tarot

- **Wands** are linked to the element of fire, which gives them enthusiasm, speed of action, communication ability, property matters, and positivity in general. Wand cards represent day-to-day activities, work and creativity.
- **Cups** are linked to the element of water, which connects them to emotions, relationships, intuition, creativity, generosity or perhaps a lack of moral fibre. Cup cards represent feelings and relating with others, along with art and music.
- **Pentacles** belong to the earth element, referring to practical matters, resources, property, wealth (or lack thereof), business, status and power. Pentacle cards represent things of value, a career and money.
- **Swords** are linked to the element of air, so they relate to ideas, communication, intellect, and professionalism. Also, dealing with problems, taking a stand and fighting back when things go wrong. Sword cards represent things that need prompt attention.
- **Court cards** often (but not always) represent people.

So, just looking at the type of cards in a spread will give you some idea of what's happening in your questioner's life.

Religion

The Tarot has nothing to do with religion. However, the images on the cards can upset religious people, so don't talk about the Tarot to religious folk, and never take Tarot cards into consecrated premises or any place connected with any religion.

Oddly enough, one religious connection does exist alongside the Tarot, and this is the Kabbalah. Some decks have Kabbalistic images, and a few readers use a Kabbalistic layout or meanings in their readings. The Kabbalah grew out of a set of ancient Jewish beliefs, but it separated from mainstream Judaism centuries ago and eventually moved into the New Age group of philosophies.

Spellcasting

Not many Tarot readers are into Wicca, but many Wiccans are into Tarot. They give readings and use cards on their altar when casting spells to make something good happen. If you are into Wicca or just into spellcasting, treat yourself to a separate deck of cards for this purpose because the intentions you put into the cards for a spell are not the same as for a reading, so you don't want your cards to become confused. You will find more about spellcasting in its own chapter later in this book.

The Tarot Journey in Colour

Psychic Training
Some Tarot readers believe it is essential to train as a clairvoyant or medium in order to read the cards really well, but those who want to read Tarot are usually intuitive anyway, and using the cards will develop this gift even more. You can meditate, join a development circle or attend a spiritualist church and learn how to become a medium. However, you don't have to do any of this because whatever route you choose, you will get something out of it.

The Chakras
You don't have to worry about opening chakras because they will snap open as soon as you do any spiritual work, but it is a good idea to close them after a day's work in the psychic field.

Closing the Chakras
The following technique comes from a medium called Barbara Ellen.

Start by imagining a light that has reached down through your body and into the earth. Turn the light off through your feet and legs until you reach the bottom of your body and the base chakra, which you can visualise as a red poppy. Close the poppy and turn off the light up to your belly button, which is the sacral chakra. This is represented by an orange marigold, which you close down. Now turn the light off up to the solar plexus chakra and close the yellow daisy. Move to the heart chakra and turn off the light, closing down a bunch of leaves in the chest area. Moving on to the throat chakra, turn off the light and close down a light blue forget-me-not. Now turn off the light up to the middle of the forehead, where you close the third eye, representing the brow chakra. Finally, turn off the light until you reach the crown chakra, where you close down a purple lotus. Send any lingering energy to the universe and ask for it to be used as healing for those who need it.

There are many ways to open and close the chakras, and many people prefer to close their chakras from the top downwards, so please use your favourite method.

1: About the Tarot

Clearing the Chakras

The following ideas came from Eve Bingham, who used to be the Secretary of the British Astrological and Psychic Society.

Imagine crystal-clear water entering your crown chakra and running through your body and out through your fingertips and toes. Focus on giving each chakra a good wash. When you have finished, close your chakras carefully.

If you get a headache while giving or receiving healing, or doing any other kind of psychic work, stop for a while. The headache suggests too much activity is going on in your upper chakras and that you need to ground yourself and balance the lower ones. You could hold a crystal in your hands for a while because crystals are linked to the earth realm, but if the weather is good, you could go outside and stand on some grass in your bare feet for a while.

If you haven't the time to close down or if you forget how to do it, this will do the trick. Imagine yourself in a purple sleeping bag that you zip up all around you, even over your head. This will strengthen your aura.

Meditating

You can meditate on one card of your choice or hold the whole deck in your hands and meditate on that. Some people find meditation very helpful, while others do not. It is a matter of personal preference.

2: Make Your Tarot Cards Work For You

Here are several topics that you may find interesting and helpful.

Reading by Images Alone

Some people have a powerful right brain that resonates with images, colour, and shapes, and these folk prefer to read cards by their illustrations rather than by learning their meanings. This is not my way of working, but let us experiment with three cards and see what their pictures can tell us.

- The first card is the Five of Wands, which looks like a friendly fight or maybe a group of people practising martial arts. This makes me think of a friendly competition.
- The second card is the Two of Pentacles, which looks like someone successfully trying to control two objects while waves lap behind him. This looks like a lot of hard work, and there may be danger from the water, or perhaps the water could offer an escape route to take him away from his problems.
- The last card is the King of Pentacles, sitting comfortably on his throne, totally relaxed and in control of his situation. He is holding a coin, and

2: Make your Tarot Cards Work for you

the scene signifies authority, representing a confident, powerful and practical man.

So, what can we make of these three cards? Perhaps this. Something starts off looking easy, but it becomes a problem until a knowledgeable and well-qualified man comes along and offers help.

Colour
Many psychic or mediumistic people get a lot of information from the colours they see on the cards. The chapter on Chakras may be helpful for this.

Key Ideas Only
If you want to learn basic card meanings but don't want to bother with much detail, go to the chapter called "Quick Clues to the Meanings of the Cards". Photocopy the page and stick it into your Tarot journal, as this will give you enough to get by.

Your Own Meanings
You can assign your own meanings to the cards, and this isn't as silly as it sounds because we all make up our own meanings to some extent.

Reading the Cards in Context
You have to read a card within the context of what is happening in your questioner's life. For instance, if your reading is about love and the cards aren't specifically related to love, you need to find a way to make sense of them.

For example, if your questioner wants to know about her chances of meeting a new lover, what would you make of the Seven of Wands in that context? Roughly speaking, this card means coping with one problem after another, but what would it say in a love context? Perhaps some difficulties must be overcome before the lady can find her handsome prince!

As you can see, context requires imagination and a touch of intuition.

Looking for a Job
Let's try the same idea with three cards again. Assume that our questioner is a woman who has been made redundant and wants to know if she will get another job, what the new job will be like and whether she will be happy there. Let's draw three cards and see how we can interpret them in the context of job-seeking.

The Tarot Journey in Colour

- The first card is the Queen of Cups, which says that a female friend or colleague will suggest a place where the questioner can look for a job.
- The second card is the Sun, which shows that the questioner will find work and that she will be happy when she does.
- The last card is the Page of Swords, which means someone will give her some helpful advice or a warning about something related to the job.

The cards suggest the questioner will find a job soon. While she will receive a warning about potential problems, the Sun is a Major Arcana card, making it especially powerful, and it predicts a happy outcome.

Picking up Clues

Context is not easy to work out when you have no idea of what is on the questioner's mind, and that is precisely the position that a professional reader is in, because clients are not about to tell the reader what is ailing them. However, this is where an overview of the cards can offer valuable clues, and the following are some ideas for you to play with:

- If the spread contains many Major Arcana cards, the questioner is going through significant events and maybe some big changes. Also, fate is in the driving seat.
- If there are very few Major Arcana cards, the questioner is in control of their own life.
- Wand cards show much rushing around, communicating, activity and creativity.
- Cup cards talk of high emotions, which may refer to a relationship matter or how the questioner feels about something.
- Pentacles indicate resources, money and business – and maybe power.
- Swords can indicate problems, things that need attention, or even things like fixing a car, engineering, cooking, and using tools.

2: Make your Tarot Cards Work for you

A Health Reading
Let us say the questioner is a man worried about his health, and we will draw one card at random and see what it tells us. The card I drew for this experiment is the Moon, which shows that something is going on that isn't apparent (it is hard to see things clearly in the moonlight), so in this case, I would suggest that X-rays and scans would be helpful. However, there is only so far you can get with one card, so you must look at the surrounding cards and see what they say.

Alternative Meanings
Cards can have several alternative meanings. I have given alternatives in the chapter on card meanings, but you will develop your own theories as time passes. This is where having a Tarot journal is worthwhile because you can jot down new ideas as they come along.

When Cards Make No Sense At All
Sometimes, a reading doesn't make any sense at all – so what is happening here? Well, maybe it isn't the right time for the client to have a reading. Don't let this get you down; just don't take money from the client. However, before you admit complete defeat, look over the spread slowly and see if something catches your attention, as this may be important. You can use a card that catches your eye to get a grip on a reading or you can use it as a significator. Lay your significator card down and lay a few cards around it to see what the significator is trying to tell you. It may work.

The Tarot Journey in Colour

Timing On the Cards
Timing events by the Tarot is very tricky and I am not sure it really works. The problem is that unlike systematical astrology or numerology, the Tarot is related to the spiritual world, and spirit doesn't understand time like we do. However, here are some ideas I have picked up over the years that you can try for yourself.

The Twelve-Month Method
Lay out twelve cards to represent the twelve months ahead and see which months contain a Major Arcana card because that will show when something important is likely to happen. Cards such as the Fool, the Magician, the Wheel of Fortune, Temperance, the Star, the Sun and the World will show times of change for the better. Difficult cards like Death, the Devil, the Hanged Man and the Tower signify months that won't be easy to live through. Use your journal to note down the cards that come up and to which months they refer, and then check the reading as the year goes by.

Days, Weeks and Months
If you are measuring something that should happen in a matter of days, lay cards out in a row until you come to a Cup card, as that will show you how many days have to pass before the event occurs. Wand cards refer to the number of weeks to pass before something happens. Pentacle cards will show you how many months have to pass, and Sword cards will predict the years that have to go by before the event occurs.

Direction on the Cards
There have been compass directions associated with the cards in the past, but the rules for this have become lost in the mists of time, so I suggest you make up your own directions and note them down in your journal. If you want a bit of inspiration, I recommend the following:

        North: Swords
        South: Wands
        East: Pentacles
        West: Cups

If your questioner is looking for a direction to travel in, say to look for romance, work, health or whatever, you can draw cards one at a time. If the first card is a Minor Arcana card, check its suit against your list of directions, but if it is a Major Arcana card, keep going until a Minor one appears.

2: Make your Tarot Cards Work for you

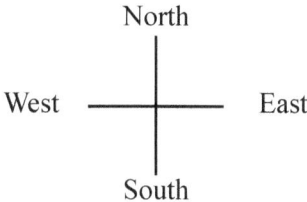

Here is another idea that you could try. Draw a cross on a sheet of paper and mark the angles North, South, East and West, then draw a card for each direction and see what comes up.

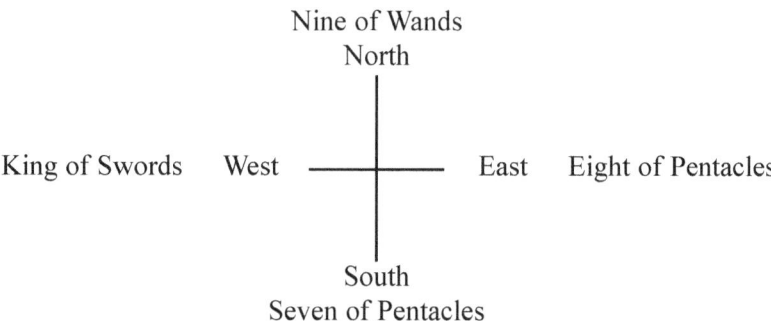

If a Major Arcana card comes up for one or more angles, it shows that direction will be important. Now, read the nature of the card to see why it is important. If a Minor Arcana card comes up, check the suit and the nature of the card to see what it says and then read the card itself. Here is a test of the system to see which direction is the most important for me.
There are no Major Arcana cards, but there is a Court card to the West that relates to an intelligent, professional man who might be challenging to handle. I have no idea who this may be, but much of the work we do is connected to the USA, which is to the West, and weirdly enough, just such a man has shown up a couple of times in readings that my friend Jackie Towers has done for me, so presumably, this man will turn up sometime in the future and for a good purpose.

The Tarot Journey in Colour

Some Extra Hints

A reading like this could throw up the following ideas for one or other of the directions:

- **Wands**: Deal with admin and communications and act if needed.
- **Cups**: A potential lover could live in this direction.
- **Pentacles**: An opportunity for business or finances.
- **Swords**: A professional connection or a chance to solve a problem.

Working Backwards

Here is something I have done from time to time for fun or when teaching the Tarot. It fascinates clients and students, so this is worth trying while developing your skills. I ask a questioner to shuffle the cards and focus on an event that happened to them in the past without telling me what it was. I then read the cards and see whether I can pick up the occurrence. If it was an emotional event, the cards should be able to pick it up.

Journals

As you can see, I have mentioned journals here and there in this book. Journalling has become fashionable, and while it may be a fad that will soon disappear, it is worth trying. The idea is to buy a notebook and write down anything interesting that you want to remember about the Tarot. Maybe draw pictures, stick in pictures from magazines, or create a mini vision board showing what you want to achieve. A really good use for a journal is to do a reading for a friend or yourself, write down the date of the reading, note which spread you use, note down the cards that came up, and write down what you thought the cards were telling you. After a few months, look at your notes again and see how accurate your reading was or where you misfired. You will discover that you were right in many cases, and even where you were wrong, you probably weren't far off the mark. Doing this from time to time builds knowledge and confidence.

Now Try Something Really Weird

Put a Tarot card face down so that you don't know what it is, then hover your left hand over the card and try to pick up the message it is giving you. Give yourself time to tune into the card before you turn it over. You are unlikely to guess what the actual card is, but you should be able to feel the nature of the energy the card is giving out and perhaps pick up what it wants to tell you.

3: Major Arcana

A Tarot deck has four suits and twenty-two extra "trump" cards, called the Major Arcana. The Major Arcana cards often point to important matters in a reading, so it is always worth carefully considering them.

Some people refer to the Major Arcana as The Fool's Journey. In this case, the Fool is young and inexperienced and he learns as he goes along. The Fool encounters each of the Tarot cards in turn and lives through the situations that come up until he has experienced everything. When we die, we reincarnate into another life and embark on another Fool's Journey.

THE FOOL

THE MAGICIAN

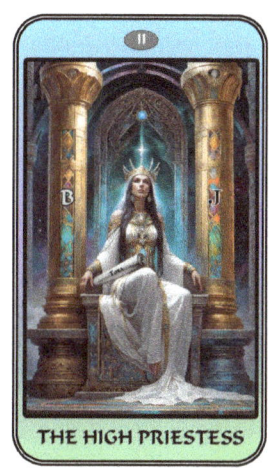

THE HIGH PRIESTESS

The Tarot Journey in Colour

0: The Fool

Key ideas: *a fresh start, a new enterprise, a new way of life.*

While looking through some ancient books on the Tarot, I saw that old-time Tarot Readers linked this card with the opening of the first book in the Old Testament, which is about the creation of the world. The book is called Genesis, and the version I remember from my Sunday school days said: "In the beginning there was nothing, then God created the heaven and the earth, and he saw that it was good." Then, the story shows how God divided day from night, eventually leading to the story of the Garden of Eden and Adam and Eve.

The Fool card represents a new situation and an entirely new set of circumstances. This card points to the start of something new, such as a job, a home, a relationship, a university course, or perhaps moving from one area to another. The point of this card is that the person has no knowledge or experience of the new setup and can only fall back on their own store of intelligence, courage, energy and ability.

The Fool is a youthful card, showing optimism and exuberance, so despite the newness of the client's situation, it doesn't usually indicate problems or worries. There is a feeling that the Fool is free of sin and that he is not tainted with anything because he has no past history, so this card suggests that the subject should move ahead with confidence. Indeed, many Tarot readers believe that when this card appears, the clients' spiritual guides will protect them as they head into a new situation and that the new venture or lifestyle has a good chance of success – or at the very least, it shouldn't be a disaster.

Extra Meanings
An element of fun is associated with this card, so it can signify a time of enjoyment. It can also denote an important journey and possibly one that is vital in some way. The Fool can bring flashes of inspiration, ideas and even spiritual messages that can put the questioner on a new road. This makes sense when we consider the astrological connections that link this card to mentality and optimism rather than fear and emotionalism.

Reversed
The Fool card is a good one to find even when reversed, but the new venture might not be as big a deal as the upright card suggests and it might not be an outright success. It would be wise to take care and not rush into anything without first looking into it.

Astrology
The Fool is associated with the element of Air, but some astrologers also assign the card to the planet Uranus

Kabbalah
Number: One
Letter: Aleph
Pathway: First, between Kether and Chockmah

The Tarot Journey in Colour

I: The Magician

Key ideas: a new venture, a new influence, a need for sales, promoting and marketing. A trickster.

This card suggests a new venture, but it is one for which the questioner already has skills, experience and knowledge to bring to the situation. The Magician can refer to starting a new business or finding a new job. It often shows up when people embark on self-employment or return to work after a few years of looking after children or caring for an elderly person. One way of expressing this is to say that the questioner is about to take a bold step. The activity may not refer to work or business, but to something like joining a committee, fund raising, putting on a play, organising a school fete or doing something for the community.

In an existing job or business, this can denote a new initiative, product, or contract and suggest an upturn in business or financial affairs. I have also noticed it turning up when life is about to become busier and when the client starts to juggle several demands simultaneously. The product or project will require promoting and marketing.

3: The Major Arcana

An element of cunning will be required, or perhaps one might say, shrewdness, because there will be some difficulties and maybe even some opposition.

The questioner will need to find ways of tackling these issues before they become insurmountable.

Extra Meanings
In some cases, this card talks of a new person coming into the questioner's life, and for someone who is hoping to meet an important new man, this can be excellent news. However, even this will probably connect with work or the subject's personal ambition.

Reversed
This can be a warning of trickery and lies around the questioner, so the subject must take care of who they allow into their life or who they work with. The problem is that the new influence may be a trickster who likes playing practical jokes or someone less than honest. Businesswise, the reversed Magician isn't a bad card, but it can mean that a promising new venture turns out to be something of a damp squib.

Astrology
The Magician is connected to the planet Mercury

Kabbalah
Number: Two
Letter: Beth
Pathway: Second, between Hether and Binah

II: The High Priestess

Key ideas: logic, intelligence, intuition needed. A teacher helps, gaining knowledge, something to be revealed.

The High Priestess, or The Priestess, as she is often called these days, is a tricky card to interpret as it has several meanings. One of the most critical interpretations refers to the questioner's attitude of mind. The questioner must take a logical and intelligent view of things and not allow emotions to overwhelm them or influence their decisions. Mental activity, analysis and brainpower will be needed, as will research and seeking the best advice. The card shows that the subject doesn't have the full picture, but something has yet to be revealed. However, intuition and instinct will also play a part, and the questioner's gut feelings should be considered.

A teacher or expert will come along and help the questioner to see what's going on. There are things that the subject needs to discover before moving forward. Among the things that may soon become clear is spiritual knowledge and the development of gifts such as spiritual healing or mediumship.

Something may be going on behind the questioner's back, and when this comes to light it may lead to a change of job, a change within a business situation or even the end of a relationship. The surrounding cards might throw some light on this matter.

Extra Meanings
The client might be doing too much for others, so they need to consider what others are demanding of them and ensure these things are not unreasonable.

One unexpected meaning that can be attached to this card is sex and sexuality. The card is so cool, so intellectual and apparently unsexy that it can hide a need that can suddenly break out and overwhelm the questioner, and this kind of overwhelming passion can lead to a difficult situation.

Reversed
The questioner is in danger of allowing emotions such as fear and anger or a powerful sexual need to overwhelm them. They may jump into something without sufficient information.

Astrology
The High Priestess is traditionally linked to the Moon

Kabbalah
Number: Three
Letter: Gimal
Pathway: Third, from Kether to Tiphareth

III: The Empress

Key ideas: abundance, fertility, femininity, well-being, moving to the countryside.

The archetypal feeling about the Empress card is of a warm, loving, feminine woman like an earth mother who is caring for a brood of happy, well-fed children. There is a feeling of sexuality here that is comforting and loving, and there is even a suggestion that the Empress is pregnant. For those hoping for an addition to the family, this card can predict the birth of a child. It can also denote the start of a good relationship or of a marriage to come. If so, it should be happy and easy rather than something filled with tension and arguments.

The Empress foretells a time of comfort, abundance and fertility, so if the client is working towards a particular goal, this should be reached. There may be a new home to come, and it should have land and space around it. This may denote a move from the city to the countryside or it may have something to do with farming. Those who love countryside pursuits or gardening will be in for a pleasant and successful time.

This is a good omen for those who are moving house, and especially those moving away from an uncomfortable or unpleasant situation to a better one.

3: The Major Arcana

Extra Meaning
Suppose the client has been struggling with life, especially if they have been coping with financial difficulty. In that case, this card shows that better times are coming.

Reversed
This shows a time of hardship, so if the subject has been overspending, it will be time to cut down on wasteful behaviour, clear debts, and stick to a budget. Projects of all kinds may be hard to get off the ground, it might be difficult to buy or sell property, and there could be financial shortages for a while. The questioner might suffer health problems relating to fertility. Indeed, the questioner might decide against getting pregnant at this time, or they may suffer a miscarriage or have a termination, while a vasectomy is another possibility.

Astrology
The Empress is associated with the planet Venus

Kabbalah
Number Four
Letter: Daleth
Pathway: Fourth, between Binah and Chockmah

IV: The Emperor

Key ideas: taking charge, a boss or father figure, practical rather than spiritual matters.

The Emperor represents a man in a good position with a strong personality. This may be a father figure, the questioner's boss, or some other male connection, but this man can be relied on. He has the knowledge, experience and willpower that will allow him to take charge of a situation.

The questioner will soon be able to exert control, make decisions, and influence whatever happens in their environment. This can denote an improvement to the questioner's career, or it can signify new work or a business situation that allows for fertility and growth. It can even refer to an event that changes the subject's life for the better. Others will respect the questioner and come to them for advice and opinions. The questioner will take control of their life. At the same time, their financial position will improve, giving them a good starting point from which to grow and develop.

If the questioner has been feeling downhearted or gloomy, this card is an indication that things will improve. It is a particularly good card to find when the subject is feeling helpless and unable to improve their circumstances, as it shows that the situation will soon change for the better.

Extra Meanings
The Emperor can denote a connection to fields such as engineering, fixing or mending cars or appliances. It can refer to precision engineering, construction, dealing with farm machinery and working at trades of all kinds.

Reversed
Someone around the client will not be reliable. If a woman hopes a particular man will be the right one, the reversed Emperor tells her the man is weak or perhaps just in a temporarily weak position. He may never finish anything he starts and may not have faith in himself, so he could become a millstone or burden to the client. The situation may be short-term, though, and the man may turn out to be all right in the long run, so perhaps the questioner should give him the benefit of the doubt.

Astrology
The Emperor is linked to the sign of Aries

Kabbalah
Number five
Letter: Hey
Pathway: Fifth, between Tiphareth and Chockmah

V: The Hierophant

Key ideas: honesty, fairness and tradition. A helpful friend, a teacher, a spiritual leader.

This card is not easy to interpret because part of its meaning is philosophical rather than referring to an event or situation.

Doing the right thing might anger friends and relatives, but the card advises the questioner to stay on the straight and narrow and avoid trouble.

Another idea is that an advisor, teacher, guru or even a spiritual guide will soon turn up and help the questioner. This might be a religious or spiritual leader or perhaps a professional person, such as an accountant, lawyer or doctor. This card is associated with listening to advice.

One good old-fashioned reading for this card is of tradition and of needing to do things traditionally, so the client should follow the conventional way of solving their problems rather than doing something original or unconventional. Another manifestation of tradition is weddings and marriage, which can occur when the Hierophant appears, so once again, tradition is a key idea in this situation.

3: The Major Arcana

Extra Meanings

Yet another meaning is that events that have been delayed will now move ahead. Contracts and documents can now be agreed and signed.

Some people see this card as an indication of psychic ability. Others see it as kindness on behalf of the questioner or of a kind person who helps the questioner.

Reversed

Tradition may not work in this situation, so the client is being advised to take an original approach and maybe to look for work in a new and unconventional field. Honesty, legality and decency will be important. Something that is going slowly will continue to take its time, which may be a source of frustration. The subject should not allow others to use them.

Astrology

The Hierophant connects with the sign of Taurus

Kaballah

Number: Six
Letter: Vau
Pathway: between Chesed and Chockmah

VI: The Lovers

Key ideas: love, romance, harmony, beauty, pleasure, but also choice and temptation.

Old Tarot cards sometimes used to depict a man with two women: the devoted, hard-working wife and the appealing temptress. Of course, the man is dithering between the two.

In my experience, the driving force is that of choice. While it may be a man trying to choose between two women, it can also emerge when a woman is considering whether to return to work or stay at home and look after the children. Frankly, whatever women do leaves them feeling guilty, so this can be a difficult choice. Sometimes, this choice is forced upon them by financial need. Another frequent scenario is a client making a major decision affecting their family. A choice may open up that means leaving a well-known and conventional way of life behind in favour of something new and exciting. A new way of life may beckon that means sacrificing security and normality in favour of adventure. This may be due to the client meeting someone to whom they feel drawn, to follow into a new life. On the other hand, they may choose to move on due to boredom or stagnation.

3: The Major Arcana

The other meaning is that true love and romance will come into the questioner's life; if so, it will be wonderful. This card can also relate to friendship, and especially to the presence of a loyal and good-hearted friend. Some colleagues may become friends, but sometimes, this simply means working with good people who create a happy, harmonious, and productive atmosphere.

Extra Meanings
A subsidiary meaning can deal with beautiful things, such as lovely clothes or artistic goods. It can also refer to making beautiful things, such as gorgeous cakes, a beautiful home or a stunning garden. If the subject needs to improve their appearance, they will now do so.

Reversed
This can denote falling for the wrong person and living to regret it. It also warns against becoming obsessed with someone or being consumed by sexual needs. The other person does not really love the questioner.

Astrology
The Lovers card is assigned to the sign of Gemini

Kabbalah
Number: Seven
Letter: Zain
Pathway: between Tiphareth and Binah

VII: The Chariot

Key ideas: victory, an effort, a journey, confusing demands.

This card talks of forging ahead and making things happen, so it can refer to an enterprise that takes energy and hard work. Something will entail the questioner putting their shoulder to the wheel, but the outcome will be worth the effort. It can indicate a battle of some kind, and it advises the questioner to have courage and not to back away from a challenge because there will be a victory in the end.

Another meaning of this card is travel, so it can denote an important journey. Sometimes, there is an advance warning that the client will need a reliable vehicle for work or for driving children around.

There may be conflicting demands on the client that make it hard for them to keep going, but the message here is to keep working towards the goal even if elements of the person's life make things difficult. Allied to this is the idea of indecision or of trying to maintain a balance under challenging circumstances. The thinking behind this is that the horses are two different colours and have two different natures. This shows that the questioner might be finding it difficult to reconcile conflicting demands, or struggling to make up their mind.

3: The Major Arcana

When Roman soldiers returned to Rome after a successful campaign, they rode through the city in chariots at the head of a parade that was called a "Triumph". A slave rode in the chariot with them, whispering in their ear, "Look not so proud, for the gods are jealous." The point was that too much self-satisfaction would upset the gods and bring bad luck.

The message for the questioner is much the same, namely, not to brag about success or possessions but to show a bit of humility.

Extra Meanings
One odd thing about this card is that it can be retroactive, showing that the battle is ongoing or that it has already been won and that it is time for the client to move on.

This can also indicate that the client will soon fix or replace their current vehicle.

Reversed
Plans won't work well and journeys will be delayed. The questioner's vehicle may not be up to the job, but the questioner may be unable to do much about this now.

Astrology
The Chariot is connected to the sign of Cancer

Kabbalah
Number: eight
Letter: Cheth
Pathway: eighth, between Geburah and Binah

VIII: Strength

Key ideas: being strong in a difficult situation, tact, and recovery from illness.

Some ancient Tarot decks and some old books give this card the number XI (11), but modern decks and books call it number VIII (8). I always call this card number VIII (8).

This card has several meanings; the first concerns coping with a difficult situation and needing patience. This can relate to a demanding job where the questioner is poorly treated and unappreciated, or it can mean being stuck in a difficult relationship from which the questioner can't escape. Frankly, it can relate to anything tiresome and exhausting. The advice is for the client to put up with the situation for the time being but to assess it from time to time and move away from it as soon as it becomes possible.

If we consider the Chinese idea of Yang and Yin, we see Yang as the assertive, courageous and enterprising masculine force, while the Yin energy is feminine in nature and, therefore, gentle, caring and able to put up with things.

3: The Major Arcana

This card represents the Yin energy, so being able to cope during trying times is important here. One might almost say, "keep calm and carry on."

The second meaning is similar: the questioner becomes seriously irritated by someone whose attitude towards the subject is disrespectful. The advice here is to use tact and diplomacy rather than letting fly with angry exchanges or obstinacy and try one's best to create a better atmosphere instead of forcing a change. If nothing can be done, the questioner must find ways in which to escape the environment.

The third meaning is much more straightforward, as this is recovery from an illness. Indeed, this is a perfect card to find if the questioner or someone around them is unwell, as it shows the person will soon be on the mend.

Extra Meanings
The questioner will need to help a sick or unhappy animal. Another meaning is to do what is right, even if those around the client are not doing the right thing.

Reversed
If the questioner or someone around them is ill, it will take time for the sick person to recover. The client might be causing problems by being bossy or misbehaving. Another possibility is putting up with a bad situation when walking away would be better.

Astrology
It's no surprise that the Strength card is associated with the sign of Leo

Kabbalah
Number: nine
Letter: Teth
Pathway: ninth, between Geburah and Chesed

IX: The Hermit

Key ideas: time out, getting away from it all, retreat and reflect, spiritual growth.

This indicates a time of retreat and reflection and a break from rushing around or being over-busy, so it says the questioner needs time to think. The Hermit could relate to anything from a quiet and restful holiday to a break from work or to working from home, or maybe the questioner should avoid socialising for a while.

This card can show that the questioner should go on an inward journey, consult a counsellor, visit an astrologer, or read spiritual books in a quest for enlightenment. This will be an excellent time for meditation, praying, walking in the countryside, daydreaming and being alone for a while. The result may be the dawning of spiritual enlightenment, a surge of psychic development or a deeper understanding of esoteric matters.

The questioner may have things to think about and problems that need to be solved, and that the questioner needs to do a lot of thinking before making decisions or taking action. Also, cool logic will be better than over-emotion at this time.

3: The Major Arcana

Extra Meanings
This may be a good time to complete a course of study or to finish outstanding jobs, especially those that the questioner needs to do alone rather than with others. It can also mean being aware that something is coming to an end.

I recently came across an unexpected interpretation of this card. My questioner was tired, and needed a holiday. The advice was to choose a restful holiday rather than their usual type, which would include lots of exploring and socialising.

Reversed
The client may refuse help from others in a difficult situation or turn away from family and friends due to fear of criticism or rejection. There may be feelings of anger or jealousy. The questioner might be waiting for a lover to come back to them, which isn't going to happen. This reversed card seems to register a waste of time and a waste of emotions. Another possibility is that the person is coming to the end of a period of retreat and reflection and is getting ready to branch out.

Astrology
The Hermit is linked to the sign of Virgo

Kabbalah
Number: ten
Letter: Yod
Pathway: tenth, between Chesed and Tiphareth

X: The Wheel of Fortune

Key ideas: change.

This card shows that nothing stays the same forever. Hopefully, the word "fortune" in the card's title signifies a change for the better. However, the card really only indicates change, and it could go in any direction. This is a classic case of looking at the surrounding cards to see what is going on and to get some idea of where the changes will arise. A point worth considering is that the change is probably down to fate rather than something the client brings about.

Extra Meanings
A period of good luck is wonderful but it never lasts, so if your finances are good at the moment, remember to put something away for a rainy day.

The questioner should not show off or become arrogant because the Wheel reminds us that life is full of ups and downs.

Reversed
I don't think this card is any different when reversed but the change may be less beneficial or slower than if the card was upright.

3: The Major Arcana

Astrology
The Wheel of Fortune is linked to the "Lucky" planet, Jupiter

Kabbalah
Number: twenty
Letter: Keph
Pathway: eleventh, between Chesed and Netzah

XI: Justice

Key ideas: balance, justice.

Some ancient Tarot decks and some old books give this card the number VIII (8), but modern decks and books call it number XI (11). I always call this card number XI (11).

Suppose the questioner is embroiled in a legal problem. In that case, the outcome will be fair, even if the questioner is not entirely happy with the decision. In a less formal setting, if someone accuses the questioner of something they didn't do, it will soon become clear that someone is lying.

Work will be fairly allocated, and friends and family will pitch in and help out rather than let the questioner do everything themselves or pay for everything themselves. If someone distributes benefits, the questioner will be given a fair share. In short, whatever the situation, justice will prevail.

The other idea is of balance, so if the questioner's life is out of balance, with too much emphasis on one side of life to the detriment of other areas , this will be rectified.

3: The Major Arcana

Extra Meanings
The questioner may become involved in a cause or a fight for someone else's rights. Another possibility is that a long-standing debt is paid - either *by* the questioner or *to* the questioner by someone else.

It is also possible that a karmic debt will soon be repaid, leaving the way clear for optimism and a happy future to evolve. In short, life will become balanced and reasonable once again.

Reversed
A fundamental injustice is likely to happen. The client must take care when dealing with official bodies and be careful if something goes wrong in the workplace. Others might be promoted over the head of the questioner, or some other injustice may occur. It may be unpleasant, but the questioner might have to apologise to make things right. The questioner may have to consider leaving a job, relationship, or family for the sake of their sanity.

Astrology
The Justice card is connected to the sign of Libra

Kabbalah
Number: thirty
Letter: Lamed
Pathway: thirty, between Tiphareth and Geburah

XII: The Hanged Man

Key ideas: delays and suspension, initiation, rites of passage, learning the hard way.

This is a tricky card to interpret as it has several meanings, none particularly pleasant or straightforward. The first and most obvious interpretation is of delay or suspension. One particular matter may be held up, and the news from the Hanged Man is probably not what the client wants to hear.

A Norse legend says the god Odin hung upside down in the World Tree for several days, when he noticed something strange among the roots. What he saw were the Runes, and as he hung there, he learned how to interpret them. This connects with the idea that the Hanged Man brings enlightenment or an increase of knowledge through personal experience and personal hardship.

There is also an admonishment to be less materialistic, more charitable and spiritual in one's outlook. In short, this isn't an easy card to deal with, but the things the questioner experiences at this time will result in a massive growth in knowledge, character and backbone.

3: The Major Arcana

Extra Meanings

The questioner will feel that fate, or perhaps other people, have taken control of their life and that they can't change a pretty desperate situation. It may even be a case of having to wait until some kind of karma has worked its way out of the client's life. Life may be put on hold due to illness; either of the subject or of those in the environment.

The good news is that nothing lasts forever, not even bad times, and that things will change for the better in time.

Reversed

A stagnant situation will now start to move forward, but one that is dying off will now come to an end. There's a warning not to make useless sacrifices, but to wait for things to improve or maybe to walk away from the situation for good.

Astrology

The Hanged Man card was traditionally associated with the element of Water, but in recent times, it has been linked to the planet Neptune

Kabbalah

Number: forty
Letter: Mem
Pathway: thirteen, between Hod and Geburah

The Tarot Journey in Colour

XIII: Death

Key ideas: transformation, an ending.

Even though most people know that the Tarot is symbolic rather than literal, there are still clients who get upset if they see this card in a reading because they wonder if it is saying that they will die soon. The Death card never predicts the death of the questioner, but it can come up when the questioner is aware that someone around them is about to pass over.

An important meaning for this card is an ending, so it shows that a situation that has been hanging on too long will now end, and the emotion the questioner will experience will be relief. Sometimes, a questioner wonders whether a relationship is truly over or whether it can be resurrected, and this card shows that it is completely finished and that it is time to move on. Similarly, this card can suggest that a failing business isn't worth keeping going or that the client will soon leave a job that isn't bringing any satisfaction. In short, anything that needs to be ended will do so. Sometimes, it even shows that a time of trouble is about to end.

Another possibility is transformation, so this card suggests that something will make the questioner change their way of life or thinking.

3: The Major Arcana

The questioner might change their appearance, redecorate their home or make some other much-needed transformation.

Extra Meanings
If the questioner has been living in cloud cuckoo land, this cards brings a dose of reality and reveals the truth.

Reversed
There are several possibilities here, with the first being that something the client hopes has come to an end is still hanging on. Another is that the questioner is trying to keep something alive that is actually finished. Either way, something needs to be ended. A somewhat old-fashioned interpretation is that the subject is misbehaving or is not doing themselves or others any good, and that a change of attitude is required.

Astrology
The Death card is linked to the sign of Scorpio

Kabbalah
Number: fifty
Letter: Nun
Pathway: fourteen, between Netzah and Tiphareth

XIV: Temperance

Key ideas: balance, moderation, harmony, peace.

This is a lovely card, but it is vague and hard to interpret. It means something like "getting things right" or "having the right recipe". The Temperance card suggests that the questioner will soon feel balanced and calm. This is a great card to find if the questioner has been through a time of trouble because it means peacefulness and a more leisurely life are ahead. It indicates that the person will put stress and strain behind them and start to enjoy life again.

Another idea is moderation, so if the questioner has been overworking, they will soon be able to ease back on their workload. If the subject has been spending more money than they can afford, there will be a time of retrenchment until debts are repaid. If the client has been drinking too much and partying too much, they will give their bodies (and their bank balances) a rest and an opportunity to recover.

If something has been troubling the questioner, they will soon see a way forward and be able to restore their peace of mind.

This card brings harmony, so if the client has been living or working in a metaphorical war zone, the rows, arguments and bad atmosphere will abate. It may mean having to leave a difficult environment, but that may be the only way to find peace and moderation.

New partnerships and connections will be pleasant, supportive, gentle and kind. Journeys will be pleasant and trouble-free.

Extra Meanings

The figure on the card usually has one foot on land and another on water, which may denote an ability to simultaneously deal with practical matters (earth) and emotional ones (water).

I have just come across another possibility, which is to allow Mother Nature to show us the right way forward.

Another really ancient interpretation is that of art, so the questioner may soon take up an artistic pursuit.

Reversed

This is a pleasant card either way up. The questioner should offload some chores and responsibilities and slow down. This is particularly the case if the client runs around after others.

Astrology

The Temperance card is associated with the sign of Sagittarius

Kabbalah

Number: sixty
Letter: Samekh
Pathway: fifteenth, between Yesod and Tiphareth

The Tarot Journey in Colour

XV: The Devil

Key ideas: being tied to something dangerous, jealousy.

A questioner may be locked into something that is clearly dangerous, and there are plenty of possibilities to choose from, such as alcohol, drugs, risky porn, gambling, belonging to a racist or terrorist organisation, or even getting involved in black magic. Another possibility is that of the client who has a wardrobe full of clothes but can't resist buying more, so whatever the story, it shows a lack of common sense.

However, most of us aren't into any of these dreadful things, so what does this card tell us? Well, we may eat the wrong things, take too little exercise or overwork because the Devil card signifies a lack of moderation. It can relate to a client who is emotionally tied to the wrong person and allowing the person to take advantage of them or abuse them.

I have often come across jealousy and envy in readings, which can be cut both ways, as it may be the questioner suffering from envy, or jealousy may be coming their way from others. Being on the receiving end of envy shows that the subject has achieved something that others envy.

Another possibility is of becoming so obsessed with something to the point where the person becomes a bore. Two classic examples are a hypochondriac who talks non-stop about their ailments or someone who has strong political views and won't shut up about them.

There is a hardness to this card, which means it talks of materialism or chasing after money or status rather than being thoughtful or helpful towards others.

Extra Meanings
The questioner can take on far too much or shoulder the burdens of others rather than allowing them to deal with their own problems.

If the questioner can see that they are their own worst enemy, they will soon break the chains that tie them to the Devil card.

There is another odd meaning to this card, which is of practicality; so, if the questioner has been living in cloud-cuckoo land and needs to develop a bit of common sense, this will happen soon.

Reversed
This card is better when reversed because it shows that the questioner can release the ties holding them back. It also indicates a development of spirituality, understanding, common sense and growth.

Astrology
The Devil card is connected to the sign of Capricorn

Kabbalah
Number: seventy
Letter: Ayin
Pathway: sixteen, from Hod to Tiphareth

The Tarot Journey in Colour

XVI: The Tower

Key ideas: an unexpected event, a shock, enlightenment.

The problem with this card is that although it predicts a shock, an upset or even a catastrophe, it doesn't explain what it will be, so it is a worrying card to find in a reading. Worse still, the shock might be large or small, so it really is a case of looking at the surrounding cards and trying to determine what is going on. Nevertheless, there are a few possibilities worth considering.

The questioner might make a mistake or do something silly that rebounds on them. However, it is equally likely that something completely unexpected will occur, and the chances are that it will cost money to put it right.

There may be some practical problem related to property or premises, so this card can show that the questioner will need to call in a plumber or builder, or they will need to replace an important appliance. A house sale or purchase might suddenly fail, or the weather may mess something up unexpectedly. Other scenarios are of a car that suddenly needs to be replaced or a computer that just stops working.

3: The Major Arcana

I have noticed that whatever the problem is, it must be addressed immediately. Also, the Tower doesn't talk about something that will happen in some distant future, but something just around the corner.

The only good thing to say about this card is that if something has been going on behind the questioner's back, they will soon know about it. And if something has been going wrong in the house, such as damp seeping into a wall or roof tiles that have become cracked, that will now come to light and need to be fixed.

Extra Meanings
There may be a family row or even a major rift, or somebody will let the questioner down.

One bit of good news is that a restrictive situation will now change and the questioner will be free to make choices and changes, and even free to walk away from a bad scene and embark on a new life.

Reversed
The only thing to say about the reversed Tower is that anything aggravating the questioner will continue to do so for a while longer.

Astrology
The Struck Tower is associated with the planet Mars

Kabbalah
Number: eighty
Letter: Peh
Pathway: twenty-seven, between Hod and Netzah

XVII: The Star

Key ideas: hope, a better future, enlightenment.

This is a lovely card to find if a questioner has been through tough times because it signifies faith in the future, hope and optimism. The Star registers a turning point for the better. Still, it is worth studying the surrounding cards to see what has held the questioner back and maybe work out how things will improve. The card also suggests that the questioner is about to develop wisdom and courage.

There is a slightly educational slant to this card, in that the client might start studying a mind, body and spirit topic such as astrology, spiritual healing, counselling, crystals or any of many mystical arts.

A period of ill health will pass and the client will feel good again. Something that has been dragging on for a long time will now come to a satisfactory conclusion. If the client has an exam looming, this is a good card to draw; in short, life will soon pick up all round, and even a good holiday may be on the horizon. Better still, the questioner will become wiser, more sensible and more efficient than before.

3: The Major Arcana

Extra Meanings
Travel is possible, so a pleasant journey may be around the corner.

Old books sometimes warned against being wasteful; this idea comes from the fact that the figure on the card is pouring water onto the land and also pouring it into a pond or river, which would presumably have been considered wasteful in days gone by.

Reversed
The questioner is being advised not to waste time, money and effort on a hopeless venture, and it can suggest that the subject is wearing blinkers and does not want to see the truth. Having said all the foregoing, this card is pretty good either way up because it foretells an improvement in the questioner's circumstances in the near future.

Astrology
The Star carries water, so it is linked to the sign of Aquarius

Kabbalah
Number: ninety
Letter: Tzaddi
Pathway: eighteen, from Yesod to Netzah

XVIII: The Moon

Key ideas: a lack of clarity, muddle and mystery.

When the Moon card appears in a reading, it shows that not all is as it seems. Moonlight and shadows make it hard to work out precisely what one is looking at, so the scenario here is of illusion, delusion, self-delusion, muddles, mysteries, insincerity and lies.

Relationships are obvious areas for muddles, especially when one person wants one thing, and the other wants something else or when one person takes advantage of another.

There can be problems at work and in business where trust between people is so important, and there could be difficulty in any situation where the client relies on someone else to do the right thing. Suppose the questioner is embarking on a new venture: in that case, this card warns them to be very careful and to perform every kind of due diligence before committing to anything. Sometimes things get screwed up for reasons nobody can prepare for, such as booking a holiday and losing it due to a strike.

A common scenario in business is that an agreement or a joint venture goes well for a few years and then suddenly collapses due to something happening in the other company that only comes to light later on. Emotions

3: The Major Arcana

rule when this card appears, with anger, unhappiness or even obsessive love in the mix.

Extra Meanings

In many esoteric systems, the Moon relates to women, especially mother figures. We see the Empress as the archetypal mother figure; however, the Moon can also play a part, so this might mean that the questioner's mother is unhappy, in trouble or about to cause trouble for others. It can also refer to a very good mother who is worried about her children.

On a more positive note, the Moon can be a creative card that talks of a growing interest in art or music or even success as a writer. It also talks of psychic or spiritual development and the growth of intuition.

Oddly enough, a clandestine love affair can be successful and enjoyable when the Moon card turns up.

Reversed

The meaning of the Moon card is much the same either way. However, when reversed, the subject is growing spiritually and becoming clairvoyant.

Astrology

Oddly enough, the Moon card isn't associated with the Moon; it links to the sign of Pisces

Kabbalah

Number: one hundred
Letter: Qof
Pathway: nineteen, between Malkuth and Netzah

XIX: The Sun

Key ideas: joy, success, children.

This is one of the best cards in the deck because it means happiness and joy. If the questioner has been ill, they will soon feel better; if there have been financial problems, these will soon be overcome. This is an excellent card for those studying or taking exams, trying to pass the driving test, or doing anything they hope will lead to a successful outcome. In business, this brings success and something to celebrate. If the questioner has been unlucky in love, a genuinely loving, unselfish and caring partner should soon come along.

There is a connection to children with this card, so it can signal the arrival of a new baby in the questioner's circle. It can also show that children in the family will be successful in school or in their hobbies and interests. They will bring glory and happiness to the family. Sometimes, there is a connection to grandchildren, neighbourhood children, teaching youngsters, getting involved in the scouting or guiding movement, or something similar. It also shows a happy and youthful attitude in general.

3: The Major Arcana

If the other cards in the reading aren't very good, this one improves the reading. It predicts a good outcome or a happy ending after a period of aggravation.

Extra Meanings
There is a possibility of travel, a lovely holiday in the sun or outdoor hobbies, such as gardening, cycling or hiking. This might even indicate that the summer months will bring a change for the better in the questioner's life.

Reversed
There may be a problem connected to children, so there might be difficulties related to pregnancy and childbirth, or a child may be sick or unhappy. It can even show up when a client opts for sterilisation, a termination or a vasectomy. Other possibilities are that life will improve but not just yet, and perhaps not with the success and happiness the questioner hopes for.

Astrology
Unsurprisingly, the Sun card links to the Sun

Kabbalah
Number: two-hundred
Letter: Resh
Pathway: twentieth, between Yesod and Hod

XX: Judgement

Key ideas: legal matters, assessing the past, something comes back to life.

This is another difficult card to interpret because it is not always clear-cut. The most straightforward aspect of the card is the legal side of things because if the questioner is involved in anything legal or official, it should go in their favour. Still, even if it does not, the outcome will be fair.

Other meanings are of the end of a phase and of looking back and assessing what has been done. For instance, if the questioner has been working on a big do-it-yourself project that is ending, they will be pleased with the result and glad to have finished it. Alternatively, the questioner may receive a bonus, a promotion and real appreciation for all that they have done in the past. If the questioner's marriage has been dying, the divorce and final agreements will soon be in place.

In short, the Judgement card represents an ending, but it will probably bring relief, a sense of a job well done or a life well-lived.

This card shows that when one phase of life ends, a new beginning will soon come into being.

If the questioner is downhearted or deflated, they can expect things to pick up again soon. There may be a new lover on the way, a new career to look forward to, a new location to move to, or anything new and better.

If an old lover comes back, it is worth giving the affair another try. However, it probably won't work out in the long run, and the questioner will eventually conclude that the relationship really is over.

Another meaning is that the client must exercise good judgement in the future.

Extra Meanings
There is a karmic feeling to this card, which shows that we earn rewards or pay debts according to our previous behaviour. It also means that life is about to speed up, and things that the questioner thought would take ages will quickly come into play. Sometimes a situation that has "died" comes alive again.

Reversed
Something that needs to come to an end is still hanging on. If the questioner hopes that an old lover will return, this will not happen.

Astrology
Tradition links the Judgement card to the element of Fire, but more recent trends connect it to the dwarf planet Pluto

Kabbalah
Number: three hundred
Letter: Shin
Pathway: twenty-one, between Malkuth and Hod

XXI: The World

Key ideas: the end of a phase of life and a new start, travel, enlightenment.

A significant phase of life is coming to an end. A change is on the way, but this is not a sudden change or even one that comes as a surprise, as it is likely to be something that has been in the air for a while. There are many possibilities here, such as a questioner finishing a training course and getting ready to put their education and qualifications to good use. Another scenario is of a career that is coming to an end.

The questioner will be pleased with the results of their efforts, and they may receive an actual award or a formal thank you from those in charge.

Love may come the client's way now, and this will bring happiness and a good future. Things are really looking up for the client when the World card appears.

3: The Major Arcana

Extra Meanings
Another possibility is travel for personal reasons or business. There may be an expansion of horizons, an increase in business or advancement in the person's career, especially if the job involves travel.

Another important aspect of this card is of opening up spiritually, which may lead to an interest in healing or becoming qualified in some form of complementary therapy, developing one's intuition and becoming a medium or even a professional Tarot reader.

Reversed
The World card means much the same either way up, but if reversed, it may signify that whatever needs to come to an end will take longer to finalise. The advice is to allow things to take their course and wait for the change that will come in time. It can mean that travel plans will be put on hold for a while, but it can also indicate that something the questioner hopes for does come about but is not as great as the client hoped it would be.

Astrology
The World card is assigned to the planet Saturn

Kabbalah
Number: four-hundred
Letter: Tav
Pathway: twenty-second, between Yesod and Malkuth

4: The Minor Arcana

The Minor Arcana is the everyday feature of the Tarot, but it can also refer to some pretty major events. The Minor Arcana of the Tarot comprises four suits, similar to those in a deck of playing cards; this isn't surprising because playing cards (and chess, for that matter) developed even earlier than Tarot. The suits are called by various names, but in this book, I use standard names that all Tarot readers know regardless of what their own deck of cards calls them. These names are Wands, Cups, Pentacles and Swords.

Other names may be:
Wands: Rods, Batons, Staves or Sceptres.
Cups: Chalices or Cauldrons.
Pentacles: Coins or Discs.
Swords: I have only ever seen these called Swords.

The connection to playing cards works like this:
Wands: Clubs.
Cups: Hearts.
Pentacles: Diamonds.
Swords: Spades.

More About the Minor Arcana

Whatever people believe about the origins of the Tarot, somewhere along the line, it became linked to the medieval and renaissance courts of Europe, and this becomes obvious when one looks at the Court cards with their Kings, Queens, Knights and Pages. Still, other decks might swap the Knights and Pages for Princes and Princesses, and different variations do exist.

- **Wands** are linked to the element of Fire, which gives them enthusiasm, speed of action, communication ability, property, and positivity in general. Wand cards represent day-to-day activities, work and creativity.
- **Cups** are linked to the element of Water, which connects them to feelings, relationships, intuition, creativity, generosity or a lack of moral fibre. Cup cards represent emotions.

4: The Minor Arcana

- **Pentacles** are linked to the element of Earth, therefore to practical matters, resources, property, wealth – or the lack of it – business, status and power. Coin cards represent resources, things of value, careers and money.
- **Swords** are linked to the element of Air, so they relate to ideas, communication, dealing with problems, loss and hardship, and taking a stance and fighting back. Sword cards represent troubles and things that need prompt attention.

The Zodiac
- Wands are linked to Aries, Leo and Sagittarius
- Cups are linked to Cancer, Scorpio and Pisces
- Pentacles are linked to Taurus, Virgo and Capricorn
- Swords are linked to Gemini, Libra and Aquarius

Court Cards Often (but not always) Represent People.
So, just looking at the type of cards in a spread gives you some idea of what's happening in your questioner's life. Even if you are a complete beginner, try to work out what it would mean if your spread contained many Cup cards. Now consider what you would make of a spread containing many Sword cards. I'm sure you are already getting the hang of this, and we haven't got very far yet!

Suits
Some people link the suits to seasons, in which case you could link Wands to spring, Cups to summer, Pentacles to autumn and Swords to winter.

The Tarot Journey in Colour

5: The Suit of Wands

The suit of Wands is associated with to the element of Fire, indicating enthusiasm, speed of action and our busy modern lives. It also relates to property, dealing with families and children, work and business, chores, household tasks, running a farm, looking after animals, having a holiday, spending time with friends, playing with pets and just about everything else we do. This suit is also linked to the idea of communication, so it can refer to travel, foreigners and foreign languages, contacting others via phone, text, email and so on, and getting around the neighbourhood. It can be associated with education and creativity, especially in writing or music.

Astrologically, this suit links to the Fire signs of Aries, Leo and Sagittarius.

These cards often link to spiritual people and spirituality in general, but also enthusiasm and sexuality.

The Tarot Journey in Colour

Ace of Wands

Key ideas:
the birth of something, a fresh start.

This optimistic card represents a fresh start after a difficult phase, showing a better outlook for the future. There could be good news for the family or good news related to a job or business project, and there are prospects for growth, development, education and success. The Ace can talk of an actual birth in the questioner's circle if appropriate, but it is often a symbolic rebirth.

Like a new plant, the new beginning can seem insignificant, but it will soon grow and develop into something substantial.

Extra Meanings

This Ace can show that the questioner will need the courage to take on a new venture, but they should avoid anything that is obviously risky.

Some Tarot readers see this card referring to the start of a relationship that has a strongly sexual element to it.

Reversed
There is still a fresh start, but it may be a while before this happens, so the questioner must be patient.

Astrology
The element of Fire and the element of Air.

Kabbalah
Kether, the crown; the first and highest sphere on the Tree of Life.

5: The Suit of Wands

Two of Wands

Key ideas:
partnership, joint ventures, caution needed.

This card tells the questioner to keep their eyes open and not expect everything to go smoothly. It often involves partnerships, doing something with others and spreading the word. This is a reasonably optimistic card, but the questioner needs to avoid putting too much trust in others. Other people have their own agendas, and this may hold something up or make it less impressive than it might otherwise be. However, there should be a good working partnership to come, although it may be a while before trust is fully established.

Part of the problem may be connected with distance, so whether business or a love affair, the partners may be at a distance. Also, the questioner should not assume the other person is as excited about things as they are.

Extra Meanings
There is an element of travel here for work or pleasure. If a change of address is in the air, this should be all right after a rocky patch.

It is possible to fall for someone still attached, but check out the other cards to see what is happening.

The questioner may soon have to deal with a proud, arrogant or impatient man.

Reversed
The situation is unclear and there may be delays and difficulties with a business or personal partnership. Property matters may be delayed.

Astrology
Mars in Aries.

Kabbalah
Chockmah, the sphere of wisdom.

The Tarot Journey in Colour

Three of Wands

Key ideas:
an improvement in affairs.

There will be an improvement in business and personal matters and a chance to get out and about and achieve a lot. There may be a new job, a promotion in the questioner's current career, or a new business enterprise to come. Travel in connection with work is likely, as is selling or marketing goods near and far. There will be cooperation, luck and happiness. Ventures that involve groups of people will be successful.

Even a new love relationship can involve a lot of running around, especially if the couple are contemplating finding a home to share.

Extra Meanings
Personal life will go well and there could be a great holiday with a partner or friend.

Three is a number associated with creativity, so the questioner might bring something new into being.

Reversed
There may be delays, or it might be better to leave things for a while before making major changes. The questioner will need more information before rushing into anything.

Astrology
Sun in Aries.

Kabbalah
Binah, the sphere of understanding.

5: The Suit of Wands

Four of Wands

Key ideas:
property matters, security, putting down roots.

This card often comes up when a questioner buys or sells property, changes their business premises, finds a new place to rent, or even rents property to others. If the subject is moving, it suggests that they will be happy in their new home. The four talks about putting down roots or creating a firm structure. If the subject is involved in a new relationship or enterprise, it should be well-founded. There is a feeling of security and success here. If the questioner wants to buy a holiday home, a caravan or just have a good holiday, this is an optimistic card to find.

Extra Meanings
The subject may create a garden or grow fruit, vegetables and trees.

This card can refer to the successful completion of a project and of a period of security to come.

Reversed
This is still a good card, but things may take longer than expected or they may be less secure than the questioner would like.

The questioner may be stuck in a boring job or be used as a household drudge by others, and they may need to look for a way out of the predicament.

Astrology
Venus in Aries.

Kabbalah
Chesed, the sphere of love.

The Tarot Journey in Colour

Five of Wands

Key ideas:
a challenge.

This is a tricky card to interpret as it suggests some kind of fight, but it isn't a serious battle or anything destructive. Indeed, the feeling here is more like a sports event, contest, or fun kickabout. It might be associated with some fund-raising events or team-building exercises that some employers put their staff through.

On a more serious note, the Five of Wands can denote a struggle that must be endured before a project gets off the ground. So, the meaning here is not to give up but to keep going because it should work out in the long run.

Tarot tradition and my own opinion are that this card does not represent a serious fight, rather perhaps something like the negotiations one has to go through before concluding a business deal or property matter. However, I have come across a very different view of this card among some modern Tarot readers. They take the card at face value, as a nasty fight that the questioner needs to win at all costs. I leave it to you to choose your own interpretation, e.g. an unimportant battle versus an important one.

Extra Meaning
If travel or other plans are delayed, the questioner will need patience. Teamwork will be needed.

Reversed
The questioner is advised not to rush into anything. Travel and other plans are likely to be delayed, and there may be legal or official matters that need attention. Issues concerning land, property, premises and so on will progress slowly.

Astrology
Sun in Leo.

Kabbalah
Geburah, the sphere of power.

5: The Suit of Wands

Six of Wands

Key ideas:
victory, achievement, relief after a trying time.

This is an excellent card to find in a reading as it signifies a victory and a sense of achievement. It can denote a breakthrough and problems being solved. Negotiations will go well, and difficulties will be overcome. If the questioner needs to impress someone, this will happen now.

Other possibilities are promotion and advancement at work, but also a good outcome after a legal battle.

Extra Meanings
The subject must avoid becoming arrogant and full of themselves.

The questioner might need a rest after a period of struggle.

Reversed
There is a battle that might not be worth bothering with, but if the questioner has no option but to fight, it will be tough. The questioner will probably win out in the end, but the effort will be tiring and aggravating.

Astrology
Jupiter in Leo.

Kabbalah
Tiphareth, the sphere of beauty.

The Tarot Journey in Colour

Seven of Wands

Key ideas:
having a lot to cope with.

The questioner has too much going on, so they must prioritise important jobs and drop the rest. There may be other people who are happy to pile their own work onto the questioner, making their life even more complicated than it is. This card can also mean having no option but to keep going until a job is finished, despite being tired and fed up.

If something is going wrong in the questioner's love life, it could be due to interference by others. If others try to push the subject into drinking too much or taking drugs, they must get away from these so-called friends.

So, whether others try to shove their chores onto the questioner or drag them into a harmful way of life, the subject will need to look after their own interests.

Extra Meanings
The questioner must look out for hidden dangers.

Reversed
There may be misunderstandings, embarrassment or some kind of mystery to cope with. The questioner is overloaded with work and can't take on any more.

Astrology
Mars in Leo.

Kabbalah
Netzah, the sphere of endurance.

5: The Suit of Wands

Eight of Wands

Key ideas:
expansion, travel.

This is an optimistic card because it means expansion of horizons, so if the client is in business, it signifies an upturn in trade, new customers, or new outlets, and with some that may be overseas. It can mean travel for business or leisure. Even if the questioner doesn't physically travel at this time, it implies they can still garner information and educate themselves.

The card represents a speeding up of affairs, so the questioner will be busy with emails, phone calls and meetings. The questioner needs to check out the other cards in the reading, as the concepts they represent will also be speeded up by the presence of the eight of Wands.

Extra Meanings
People may come into the questioner's life from a distance, including new friends or even an important new lover.

These things may happen almost overnight, due to the speed factor of this card.

Reversed
Travel plans may be delayed or cancelled, and business will not go well. It would be better to wait for a while before starting new ventures.

Astrology
Mercury in Sagittarius.

Kabbalah
Hod, the sphere of majesty.

Nine of Wands

Key ideas:
not all problems have been solved.

Most of the questioner's problems are behind them. However, the questioner will need to take a cautious attitude because there is still something that is not quite right. The client may feel that they are in a position of security, but they should still keep their wits about them in case something unexpected comes up, or a few things go wrong.

If life is stressful at the moment, the questioner can take heart because this card indicates that problems will soon be solved, and a particular job will soon be satisfactorily completed. The client should keep going, because they are in a very good position and will soon be content with their progress.

Extra Meanings
The subject is fatigued after a period of hard work, so they need to recharge their batteries.

Reversed
The questioner needs to be cautious and not take anything at face value. They should learn to be flexible and not dig in their heels, because obstinacy will not solve anything at this time.

Astrology
Moon in Sagittarius.

Kabbalah
Yesod, the sphere of foundation.

5: The Suit of Wands

Ten of Wands

Key ideas:
burdens, lots to do.

The questioner will be overloaded with jobs and mustn't volunteer for any more, or they will become ill. Extra responsibilities can be welcome if they lead to job advancement, but there has to be a limit. If the family tries to lumber the client with looking after their children or with other responsibilities, the questioner will need to work out their priorities and drop less important things.

There is light at the end of the tunnel, though, and the end of a heavy task is in sight.

Extra Meanings
Sometimes, travel comes into the picture with this card, either for family purposes or for business. While it can be arduous, it would eventually be worth it.

Reversed
On the one hand, promotion and a salary increase are not on the cards right now, but the good news is that the questioner's workload at home and work will soon ease.

Astrology
Saturn in Sagittarius.

Kabbalah
Malkuth, the sphere of the kingdom, signifying the earth.

The Tarot Journey in Colour

Page of Wands

Key ideas:
communications, an energetic youngster.

As a person, this card represents a lively child or a youngster of either sex. The child is restless and keen to be out and about with friends.

The questioner might soon have visitors, and if so, they will be young at heart and fun. Good news is on the way, and if the subject is waiting for news about property or business, it should arrive soon. Sometimes, this refers to writing as part of a job or even success in writing or broadcasting.

Extra Meanings
There may be good news soon, about friends and loved-ones.

Reversed
Delays are in evidence and they might have something to do with a young person. There may be delays and setbacks in connection with educational matters. There may be postponements in other areas of life, such as business or getting something done around the home. Bad news may be on the way.

Astrology
The sign of Sagittarius

Kabbalah
There is no Kabbalistic connection for this card.

5: The Suit of Wands

Knight of Wands

Key ideas:
movement of affairs, a lively young man.

As a person, this represents a man below middle age who rushes into the questioner's life. He should be honest and reliable, and he will have interesting news and information to impart. This may be a lover, a friend or a business connection. He will be fun, even if he isn't around for the long haul.

As a situation, this means moving forward quickly with lots of communication, travel, and even a change of address. There may be a visitor from overseas.

Extra Meanings
As a person, this Knight is brave, generous and good-hearted. He has overcome many obstacles in his life.

As a situation, the questioner may make changes very quickly and without much thought before doing so.

Reversed
A young man may be insincere or even a liar. Nothing will move as quickly as the questioner would like, and something important may be stuck on the back burner for a while.

Astrology
If you would like to link the Court cards to astrology, this person would have the Sun or ascendant in Sagittarius.

Kabbalah
There is no Kabbalistic connection for this card.

Queen of Wands

Key ideas:
a strong woman, business becomes important.

Tradition says this is a capable businesswoman with leadership qualities and an aura of success. She is reliable and competent, a good communicator and a good friend. However, she doesn't have as much confidence as her outer manner suggests, so she should avoid bullies or those who make hurtful remarks.

This Queen is affectionate, loving and strongly sexed. She may not be an earth-mother type, but she ensures that her family is well cared for. The Queen is also fond of animals or good with practical things such as sewing, craftwork, gardening or cooking. She is often quite lucky.

As a situation, this card predicts success in a career and business or any kind of buying, selling and negotiating.

Extra Meanings
The questioner must listen to their own voice and not take too much notice of the opinions of others.

Reversed
This woman may have too much on her plate, or she may mean well but not be able to come up with the goods. In short, she is not entirely reliable and may not fulfil her promises.

Astrology
If you want to link the Court cards with astrology, this Queen will have the Sun or ascendant in Leo.

Kabbalah
There is no Kabbalistic connection for this card.

5: The Suit of Wands

King of Wands

Key ideas:
an intelligent man, negotiations.

This is a cheerful man and a great companion, but he may not be reliable. He may enjoy gambling or having such a good time that he spends too much money on fun things. He is generous, kind and fine as long as the questioner doesn't rely on him too much. He is a good teacher, a good communicator and a good listener. He is a good friend who means well and wants to be supportive, but he may not be as strong as the client would like him to be.

KING OF WANDS

Extra Meanings
The questioner will gain knowledge, experience and wisdom.

Reversed
It isn't a good idea to rely on this man too much or believe everything he says. He may mean well, but he may be too busy or have too much going on in his life to be much use to the questioner.

Astrology
If you want to link the Court cards with astrology, this King will have the Sun or ascendant in Aries.

Kabbalah
There is no Kabbalistic connection for this card.

The Tarot Journey in Colour

6: The Suit Of Cups

The suit of Cups is linked to the element of Water, so it suggests strong feelings. To be sure, this suit looks at love and partnerships, but it talks of an emotional response to anything the questioner has going on, whether at work, in the family, with neighbours and much else. The Cup cards will show where the emotions are being overstimulated and point to areas where the person needs to calm an emotional situation.

This suit can mean studying, so it might refer to education or training in a formal sense. Still, it can also suggest the development of spirituality, intuition and the ability to feel what is happening in the environment. Cups also connect to beauty, music, and the arts. Being so linked to the feelings, it can mean thinking with the heart rather than the head.

Astrologically speaking, the Water connection means these cards are especially associated with the signs of Cancer, Scorpio and Pisces.

Ace of Cups

Key ideas: a gift, a new romance.

A traditional meaning for this card is a lovely gift or even an engagement ring, and it can mean falling in love with someone new. However, this card can also refer to a new friendship and a happy and cheerful social life. If the questioner is already in a good relationship, it suggests that this will continue to be happy, and maybe even improve further as time passes. This card can predict a new baby coming into the questioner's circle, or it may foretell some other happy event. Like all Aces, this suggests the start of something, which in this case would be a happy phase of life.

Extra Meanings
These subjects may treat themselves to something nice. The client may become over-emotional or obsessive.

Reversed
This is not turning out to be the great love affair that the questioner is hoping for, or it could suggest romance that is still some way off in the future. It is a pleasant omen for social life, and a small but welcome gift may come to the questioner.

Astrology
The element of Water and the planet, Neptune.

Kabbalah
Kether, the sphere of the crown.

6: The Suit of Cups

Two of Cups

Key ideas: true love, a good friendship.

If the questioner is in a happy relationship, it will continue to be good, and if they are hoping to meet someone new, the outlook is also good because this is an excellent card for love and happiness. It can mean making up after an argument or perhaps returning to an old lover. However, it also denotes friendship, affection and good working relationships.

The questioner's social life will pick up and there will be a lot of fun in the near future.

Extra Meanings
A business partnership will work well and be enjoyable.

Reversed
This can refer to a parting that may go as far as a divorce. On the other hand, it may simply be a matter of one partner having to go away for a while due to their job or for some other practical reason. The questioner should not hope for too much from other people at this time.

Astrology
Venus in Cancer.

Kabbalah
Chockmah, the sphere of wisdom.

The Tarot Journey in Colour

Three of Cups

Key ideas: celebration, women getting together.

This lovely card signifies a celebration, which could be something in the family, among friends or at work. It can indicate a birthday, a Christmas party, a wedding, celebrating a new baby or anything else that is nice. It can also denote a women's gathering or a girly weekend with friends.

There will be reunions and maybe reconciliation if the client has fallen out with a friend or relative.

Extra Meanings

If the questioner hopes for a good life with a loving partner, this is a great card to find.

Reversed

At worst, this can indicate a split and even a divorce, but it can also predict a fun-filled love affair that doesn't stand the test of time. Friends may fall out, and a group of people may disperse when a project comes to an end. In a more straightforward vein, the reversed Three of Cups can mean a night out at a café or a disco, a one-night-stand or some other pleasant event that is not particularly long-lived or especially memorable.

Astrology

Mercury in Cancer.

Kabbalah

Binah, the sphere of understanding.

6: The Suit of Cups

Four of Cups

Key ideas: dissatisfaction.

While many things are going right in the questioner's life, something is still missing, and the client may feel that the grass must be greener elsewhere. The questioner may not even know what they want, only that they don't have it! Maybe the questioner should focus on the good things they already have, not on what they think they lack.

The questioner may be bored with their life at present and yearning for adventure or excitement.

A relationship may have become stale and too mundane.

Extra Meanings
Another meaning is an opportunity or advancement coming to the questioner from out of the blue. (I saw a man on the TV saying this, and I thought it was an excellent alternative interpretation for this card.)

Reversed
This card shows that new friends or colleagues will make the questioner's life happier. It also indicates acceptance of current circumstances rather than longing for things that are out of reach.

Astrology
The Moon in Cancer.

Kabbalah
Hesed, the sphere of love.

Five of Cups

Key ideas: loss, sadness, having to make a fresh start.

This miserable card represents loss and sadness, but not all is lost. The questioner will soon be able to move away from a rotten situation and make a fresh start, having learned a few hard lessons along the way. The advice is for the questioner to pick themselves up and work towards a better future.

The client may need to leave a bad situation and get away from toxic and destructive people, as this would open the door to a brighter future.

Extra Meanings
Something hasn't worked out well, but there is no point in looking back to the past and being resentful, because there will be new things in the future to forward to.

Reversed
A bad time is coming to an end, and the questioner is coming to terms with what happened. New friends and new opportunities are around the corner.

Astrology
Mars in Scorpio.

Kabbalah
Geburah, the sphere of power.

6: The Suit of Cups

Six of Cups

Key ideas: back to the future.

This is an awkward card to interpret because it includes so many possibilities. I have found it talking about family gatherings or celebrations that bring the questioner into contact with those whom they haven't seen for a long time. However, the main idea is to look back and resurrect the past in some way, so it may mean catching up with old business associates, reviving a skill that the subject hasn't used for a long time, maybe getting the old photo albums out or talking to friends about the past.

Extra Meanings
There is a feeling of pulling backwards in order to move forwards here. Something from the past should soon bring luck and opportunities.

Sometimes, this means using one's life experience to help young people or spending time with children and young people.

Reversed
The questioner is being advised to forget the past and move on because nothing will be the same as it was. A family gathering may be disappointing, and family members or old friends will be unhelpful. On the plus side, a new lover or lifestyle are on the way.

Astrology
The Sun in Scorpio.

Kabbalah
Tiphareth, the sphere of beauty

The Seven of Cups

Key ideas: too many options, new love.

The questioner has many options, but it is hard to see which is right, and there is no clear direction. One solution is for the questioner to meditate and see if something bubbles up from their subconscious. Some crystals are good for bringing clarity, so the questioner might consider obtaining one of those and keeping it in their pocket for a while.

Even if these activities don't give an immediate answer, coincidences, pointers and feelings will provide some guidance. Another idea is for the questioner to let time pass, go with the flow and make no major decisions until the mist starts to clear.

Extra Meanings
Another interpretation is that if money matters have prevented a love affair from moving in the right direction, this will soon be put right.

Reversed
This card is actually better when reversed because it shows that clarity is on the way and muddles will soon vanish.

Astrology
Venus in Scorpio.

Kabbalah
Netzah, the sphere of endurance.

6: The Suit of Cups

Eight of Cups

Key ideas: daylight follows night.

It will take courage and perseverance to get through this phase, but the misery won't last much longer. The questioner feels as though they are walking through the dark night of the soul, but the fact is that most of their troubles are behind them, the worst is over, and there will soon be plenty to look forward to.

This card shows a figure plodding through a hilly area at night, and this might be quite real, as the questioner may soon need to take an important journey. It can also mean going on an inward journey in order to analyse a situation before making any changes.

Extra Meanings
An old Gypsy interpretation says that a fair-haired woman will soon help the questioner, and as daft as this may sound, I have often found this to be true.

Reversed
The bad times will soon be over, and there will be fun and laughter in the near future.

Astrology
Saturn in Pisces.

Kabbalah
Hod, the sphere of majesty.

Nine of Cups

Key ideas: satisfaction.

The subject will soon be happy and satisfied with life. Still, they mustn't show off about their good fortune, become smug or consider themselves to be super-clever.

The questioner is in for a really good time, because their social life will improve and there will soon be new friends with whom to have fun. If the client likes holidays in good hotels or maybe cruises, these could soon be on the horizon. Whatever happens, there are joyful times ahead.

In times gone by, this used to be called the "wish card" because it predicts a time of joy and happiness.

Extra Meanings
An old traditional meaning says that marriage to an older person might be coming.

Reversed
Although things are going well, setbacks may occur before reaching the goal. For instance, the questioner my take a driving test, fail and then retake it and pass. Minor problems will soon be solved.

Astrology
Jupiter in Pisces.

Kabbalah
Yesod, the sphere of foundation.

6: The Suit of Cups

Ten of Cups

Key ideas: happiness, success.

This shows great joy and a happy time with family and friends. There is love, happiness, fun, success and pleasure in every aspect of life.

Although the Ten of Cups is especially concerned with happiness in the family, it can also refer to financial gain and future property.

Even a new romance can appear here, and, if so, it will be successful.

Extra Meanings
This card brings great news for the family and for joyful celebrations with loved ones.

Reversed
This is a confusing card because it has several potential meanings. The first is that happiness and joy are on the way but not right now, while the second meaning is that the happy events will be okay but not spectacular. Then, there are possibilities of family rifts and even a split between members of a family or the breakup of a relationship. The reader needs to check out the surrounding cards to see what is really going on here.

Astrology
Mars in Pisces.

Kabbalah
Malkuth, the sphere of the material universe.

Page of Cups

Key ideas: *a gentle youngster, study, information.*

As a person, this can be a child or young person (often female) who is artistic, gentle and kind but also lazy, or in need of encouragement.

As a situation, this card is about learning new things or gaining information. This could predict a course of study, a period of research or just gathering information. There is a connection to art or music here, or some other kind of creative endeavour.

Extra Meanings
Business matters need investigation before the questioner plunges in. Another meaning is of good news. The questioner may soon fall head over heels in love.

Reversed
Studies will be arduous and long-winded. There may be trouble concerning a baby, child or young person. Someone is likely to behave like a fool.

Astrology
The elements of both Earth and Water are associated with this Page.

Kabbalah
There is no Kabbalistic connection for this card.

6: The Suit of Cups

Knight of Cups

Key ideas: a romantic man, overseas travel.

As a person, this is a charming man who is below middle age. He is great company and a good lover, but he is probably better as a friend than a partner in the long run. He has a great sense of humour and a kind heart, but when he is in the wrong mood, he can be unpleasant. This card can show that a new lover is coming along and that he will be gentle, kind and lots of fun but not exceptionally reliable in the long run.

All Knights can denote travel and movement, and as the suit of Cups is associated with water, this may suggest crossing water. It can bring changes in business or among the people the questioner has typically around them.

Extra Meanings
Art and music are indicated, so it might denote a job in those fields.

Reversed
A love affair may cool off or even come to an end. A man is unreliable, moody and difficult at times. He may be selfish, weak, or a cheat in matters of love or money. At best, this is a man who is all right in himself, but he is not in a position to give the questioner the relationship they want. Care should be taken in matters of love and romance.

Astrology
If you like astrology, this Knight can represent someone with the Sun or ascendant in Pisces.

Kabbalah
There is no Kabbalistic connection for this card.

Queen of Cups

Key ideas: a loving woman, a good listener.

QUEEN OF CUPS

This kind and loving woman is good with children and animals. She would make a good wife and a wonderful friend, and has a terrific sense of humour. She is also highly sexed, but she can be moody and materialistic. She may be into the arts, design, crafts or music.

As a situation, this means a pleasant time, but not one in which anything significant happens, except perhaps in the area of love and romance.

This card can indicate a growing interest in dancing and music, so the questioner might take up these hobbies in the future.

Gardening or making a water feature in the garden are also possibilities at this time.

Extra Meanings
This lady is a good listener, so others tend to use her as a counsellor.

Reversed
This lady may appear friendly, but she is unhelpful and unreliable. She can be more interested in getting things for herself than doing much for others.

Astrology
If you are into astrology, this Queen could have the Sun or ascendant in Scorpio.

Kabbalah
There is no Kabbalistic connection for this card.

6: The Suit of Cups

King of Cups

Key ideas: a wonderful friend, holiday romance.

This King would make a wonderful friend because he is helpful, intelligent and creative. He may be a good businessman, but he may not be totally honest in business. He is highly sexed and a clever lover, but he isn't great husband material as he may find it hard to stay faithful to one person. Very affectionate, but he can be moody and possessive, immature and idle. He is, however, very intuitive.

Extra Meanings
As a situation, this can suggest a holiday romance, a nice trip, an artistic or creative endeavour, the start of psychic development or the growth of intuition.

Reversed
This may signal a love affair that is losing momentum. As a person, the King may be kind and affectionate. However, he may not be able to be with the questioner full-time, either because he is married or due to the pressure of his job. He may be possessive, moody and challenging at times, a loser in life and love or he could even be on the receiving end of someone else's fixation.

Astrology
If you are into astrology, this King could have the Sun or ascendant in Cancer.

Kabbalah
There is no Kabbalistic connection for this card.

The Tarot Journey in Colour

7: The Suit Of Pentacles

The suit of Pentacles is linked to the element of Earth, so it is concerned with practical matters. It relates to resources, property, business, finances, goods and services. This suit can define a person's status, wealth and position in the community, but it can also refer to professional people who deal with financial matters on behalf of others. It can concern large purchases, such as land, property, farm machinery and vehicles, and such things as mortgages, bank loans, shares and so on.

Negatively, this can talk of materialism, selfishness and greed, even in the sense of eating and drinking too much!

The astrological connection is with the Earth signs of Taurus, Virgo and Capricorn.

Ace of Pentacles

Key ideas: a new source of income or a gift.

Aces always mean something new; in this case, it can mean a new source of income or an increase in income, which may even refer to a windfall. It may signify a gift or goods that are worth something to the questioner, although not necessarily in the monetary sense. A letter, email or other communication may bring good news about financial matters.

Extra Meanings
The Ace of Pentacles could denote a new and better-paid job.

Reversed
There should be a small windfall, a small raise, a small bonus, or something good regarding work and business matters.

It isn't a good time for the questioner to get into risky or speculative ventures, as these will struggle to succeed.

Astrology
The planet Pluto and the element of Earth.

Kabbalah
Kether, sphere of the crown.

7: The Suit of Pentacles

Two of Pentacles

Key ideas: juggling time and money, a parting.

The traditional idea here is of borrowing from Peter to pay Paul because there may not be enough money to cover all eventualities. What usually happens is that there is just about enough for the necessities but nothing left over for luxuries or even for an occasional night out on the town. The Two of Pentacles can refer to being short of time rather than money and trying to cope with several demands that are all going on at the same time.

Extra Meanings
This card can indicate a divorce or a split, with the dividing up of goods and property that follows. It could even denote a collapse of a business partnership where the various parties go their separate ways.

Reversed
A working partnership might end, but this may simply be because the job or project has run its course. Otherwise, this talks of an easier time with less work to do and fewer money worries.

Astrology
Jupiter in Capricorn.

Kabbalah
Chockma, the sphere of wisdom.

The Tarot Journey in Colour

Three of Pentacles

Key ideas: a job to be done, renovating property.

The idea here is of a questioner being given a particular job to do, which allows the subject to use their skills and knowledge and earn some money. The questioner is talented and possibly qualified in a particular trade or skill, and others will be happy to employ the subject.

A business may be hired to work for another business as a sub-contractor.

Extra Meanings

The card can turn up when a questioner moves house and has work that needs to be done or when the client decides to extend, renovate or improve their current abode.

Reversed

A project may be too big or complicated to accomplish, and the client may decide to turn it down, or they may do it but then struggle to finish it. Perhaps there is a deadline that is too tight.

Astrology

Mars in Capricorn.

Kabbalah

Binah, the sphere of understanding.

7: The Suit of Pentacles

Four of Pentacles

Key ideas: an improvement in income, but a warning against greed.

The questioner will soon see an improvement in their income, which could bring real financial security. However, the questioner should not push any luck that comes their way down the throats of others by becoming materialistic, selfish or smug.

Some Tarot readers see this as bringing long-term benefits, while others feel it represents a welcome windfall but not permanent wealth.

Extra Meanings
It would be silly to rush out and spend the money without keeping some of it back for a rainy day.

The questioner should not become greedy or hard-hearted.

Reversed
Money will be tight, and payments may not come in on time. The questioner might falter in a job or fail an exam.

Astrology
The Sun in Capricorn.

Kabbalah
Chesed, the sphere of love.

The Tarot Journey in Colour

Five of Pentacles

Key ideas: *poverty, loss, but there is an answer somewhere.*

The image on most decks shows a family trudging through snow and struggling to survive, and this isn't surprising because most Fives are difficult cards. The card tells the questioner that they will experience a tough patch where they will go through financial loss and hardship.

However, they might find an answer if they look for a different way of earning an income, because they seem to be banging their head on a brick wall by sticking to the same old routine.

Extra Meanings
Oddly enough, this card can indicate an intense love affair. However, it isn't likely to work out well in the long run, so the questioner will feel lost and lonely for a while. Perhaps the client is looking for love in all the wrong places or choosing partners who are guaranteed to disappoint them.

Reversed
This card is much better when reversed, as it shows that a time of loss and hardship is coming to an end. Fun and pleasure are coming, but it will be a while before this happens.

Astrology
Mercury in Taurus.

Kabbalah
Geburah, the sphere of power.

7: The Suit of Pentacles

Six of Pentacles

Key ideas: giving to charity, paying debts.

This is a tricky card to interpret. A traditional meaning for this card was to give charity to those in need, but in modern terms, it means that the questioner will soon have to dole out money. This may be a case of paying taxes, clearing debts, paying school or college fees, financing a divorce settlement or helping family members who have fallen on hard times. Indeed, the questioner may feel that money is pouring out through their fingers.

However, the questioner might not be the one paying out money, because it might be coming in to them; the subject may receive money due to a divorce settlement, a benefit allowance, a pension, or some other way. Either way, the questioner will have money to spend, but who pays for what needs to be addressed.

Extra Meanings
The questioner may have a friend or relative who needs help, and if so, they should do so.

Reversed
This is similar to the upright version, but the outpouring of money will soon end.

Astrology
The Moon in Taurus.

Kabbalah
Tiphareth, the sphere of beauty.

Seven of Pentacles

Key ideas: hard work, but the rewards are worth it.

The questioner is working hard on a particular project, and it will take time and effort to complete it, but the job will be successful in the long term.

This card is especially linked to long-term projects, therefore to projects that take time to come into fruition. There are many possibilities, and farming is one because it takes time for crops to grow or for animals to mature.

Other projects might be putting on an event such as a play or an annual fashion show. As I know all too well, it takes time and effort to write a book, so that would also fit into this kind of long-term category.

Extra Meanings
The card shows that the subject is getting tired, so a rest will soon be needed.

Reversed
A phase of hard work will soon end, but if a job proves to be more trouble than it is worth, it may be best to drop it.

Astrology
Saturn in Taurus.

Kabbalah
Netzah, the sphere of endurance.

7: The Suit of Pentacles

Eight of Pentacles

Key ideas: lots of work to be done.

If the questioner is looking for work, this is an excellent card as it shows there will soon be plenty to do. It can indicate a raise in wages, a promotion or some other improvement in the client's career. Sometimes, the client learns a new skill or a new way of doing things, but whatever the scenario, it is a good one, as others will respect the questioner for their ability and their work ethic, and extra money will soon follow.

Extra Meanings
Education is an important issue here, because the questioner may need to obtain specific qualifications, or perhaps to work through an apprenticeship before they can move forward.

Reversed
This represents a frustrating situation because it means that work will not go as well as the questioner would like. If the work is okay, the project may simply be reaching its natural conclusion, and the questioner will have to look for something new or even learn how to do something completely different.

Astrology
The Sun in Virgo.

Kabbalah
Hod, the sphere of majesty.

The Tarot Journey in Colour

Nine of Pentacles

Key ideas: home improvements, creating a garden.

This card suggests that money will come in soon, so the client may receive a legacy, a bonus or a windfall. The questioner will probably spend the extra cash on buying or improving a property or premises, so there might be a new home, or perhaps a new kitchen, a home extension or other renewals.

If the work is not as ambitious as this, it will still mean improving the décor and look of the home. One thing I have found when this card comes up is that the client does something about the floor, so it may mean putting down wooden flooring or buying new carpets and rugs.

Extra Meanings
This card has an outdoorsy feel, so it can refer to creating a garden or it may talk of a questioner who decides to grow their own vegetables and fruit.

Reversed
There are two possibilities here: the first is having to sell goods to clear debts, and the second is having a clear-out. For instance, a client who plans to set up as a therapist will need to clear out a room in their home to create a consulting room for their patients.

Astrology
Venus in Virgo.

Kabbalah
Yesod, the sphere of foundation.

7: The Suit of Pentacles

Ten of Pentacles

Key ideas: success and wealth.

This is a great card as it foretells a good income and a comfortable way of life. A work project or business idea will take off and bring long-term results. A family will be in a good position, and the benefits of the hard work that everyone has put in will last, possibly for several generations. There may be travel in connection with business.

The questioner might find a life partner and the union will stand the test of time. The couple will be comfortably off, and the hope is that the marriage will be happy. However, it may be a good idea to check out surrounding cards to see if they agree with this. There could be children to look forward to or even the foundation of some kind of dynasty.

Extra Meanings
This card can refer to inherited talents or family values. It can also refer to a growth of spirituality and happiness that is not directly related to money or business.

Reversed
Money and success are on the way, possibly in the form of a pension or a small income. There may be a gift or a windfall, but this will not be a life-changing amount.

Astrology
Mercury in Virgo.

Kabbalah
Malkuth, the sphere of the Kingdom.

Page of Pentacles

Key ideas: a practical youngster, news about goods or money.

PAGE OF PENTACLES

As a person, this page is a sensible or reliable child or young person. The youngster is practical and capable, and there may be good news about the youngster.

There may be news about business, about something the questioner is trying to achieve, or finances. There may be a journey over land concerning business or promotion and a salary increase. This card is a good omen for financial matters.

Extra Meanings
The questioner might win a raffle or have some other kind of windfall.

Reversed
A youngster might have problems, but these should be reasonably easy to sort out. As a situation, this could be good news about business or money, or it could refer to a delay or setback that will take time to clear. Any payments that are due could take time to do so.

Astrology
The element of Earth.

Kabbalah
There is no Kabbalistic connection for this card.

7: The Suit of Pentacles

Knight of Pentacles

Key ideas: a young businessman, business and travel.

This could relate to a person who is connected to work, business or money matters, so if the questioner is dealing with builders, workers or delivery people, this person would be helpful.

As a situation, this shows movement in affairs that bring luck with anything to do with work, business, dealing with tradespeople or buying and selling things. It can predict travel in connection with work.

Extra Meanings
This card can refer to a harvest or the completion of a project.

Reversed
Someone may not be able to help the questioner, or they may be unreliable. They may rush out of the questioner's life just when they are most needed. As a situation, this can bring mild benefits, while travel will only produce mediocre results.

Astrology
If you are into astrology, this Knight may have the sun or ascendant in Capricorn.

Kabbalah
There is no Kabbalistic connection for this card.

Queen of Pentacles

Key ideas: a businesslike woman, good news about money.

As a person, this card represents a plump woman with lots of dark or reddish hair. She is probably good at admin and should be a reliable and capable worker. She may tend to worry about money, even if she is financially secure. She is a good negotiator. On the personal side, she is a loving and affectionate partner and a good friend.

As a situation, this card shows a settled phase with enough money for life to be peaceful. It indicates a combination of luck and the questioner's own common sense.

Extra Meanings
This Queen can be moody and sometimes a little selfish.

Reversed
There may be a selfish, materialistic woman around the questioner, or she may be all right but temporarily down on her luck. As a situation, this shows setbacks or delays in financial or business matters.

Astrology
If you are into astrology, this Queen may have the Sun or ascendant in Virgo.

Kabbalah
There is no Kabbalistic connection for this card.

7: The Suit of Pentacles

King of Pentacles

Key ideas: A man who deals with finances.

This could be a well-built middle-aged man with dark or grey hair. He is a father figure who may have advice to offer the questioner. He is conservative, sensible, practical and reliable and could work in banking, accountancy or business. He is a family man who loves his children and grandchildren.

As a situation, this shows a good phase regarding finances, resources and practical matters. If the questioner is buying a home, a car, or some other large item, it will be worthwhile. Investments will pay off, and there will be money luck.

Extra Meanings
The questioner will need to act quickly and decisively in the near future.

Reversed
A man may look good but turn out to be a loser, an abuser or against the questioner in some way. He can't be trusted. As a situation, the card warns the questioner not to take chances or invest unwisely.

Astrology
If you are into astrology, this King may have the sun or ascendant in Taurus.

Kabbalah
There is no Kabbalistic connection for this card.

The Tarot Journey in Colour

8: The Suit Of Swords

This suit is linked to the element of Air, an intellectual element filled with knowledge, thoughts, concepts, conversation and sometimes travel. This is the most challenging of the four suits because the cards talk of serious matters that can't be ignored.

Some Sword cards talk about health problems and even surgery, while others refer to financial difficulties, business struggles or a relationship that is in trouble, and they can suggest that the questioner would be better off leaving a person or a situation. Sword cards can be viewed as karmic, because they help the questioner to clear their karmic debts.

Sometimes, Sword cards show where professional help is needed, such as doctors, lawyers or other experts. However, this suit can also talk about contracts, deals and arrangements, and such things as heavy jobs, building or some form of metal work.

Swords link to the Air signs of Gemini, Libra and Aquarius.

The Tarot Journey in Colour

Ace of Swords

Key ideas: new ideas, things can only get better.

ACE OF SWORDS

Aces always mean something new, and this one can signify a new idea, a new concept, and even a new look if the questioner feels the need for it. The Ace represents taking control into the questioner's own hands, so if the client needs to get a grip on something, they will do so. If life is challenging, this card should give the questioner tools with which to cope. Everything will happen quickly now.

Extra Meanings
Swords are double-sided, so there is a warning here against being aggressive or selfish.

Reversed
A job may go south, a business may collapse, a betrayal may come to light, or a health problem may emerge. The questioner will need to take care and be vigilant.

Astrology
The element of Air and the element of Fire.

Kabbalah
Kether, the sphere of the Crown.

8: The Suit of Swords

Two of Swords

Key ideas: not seeing the wood for the trees.

This card is not easy to interpret because it shows that the questioner is in the dark. It may be so difficult to see straight that the only answer is to meditate and ask for spiritual guidance. It's also worth looking at the surrounding cards to see what they have to say.

Extra Meanings
It's possible that the client needs to face up to reality but is unwilling to do so. Maybe the questioner cannot make the changes that need to be implemented.

Oddly enough, this card can indicate a settlement, a peace treaty or a meaningful agreement.

Reversed
This card is better when it is reversed because it brings a stalemate to an end and allows the questioner to act and move on. Travel, agreements and changes for the better are all possible now.

Astrology
The Moon in Libra.

Kabbalah
Chockmah, the sphere of wisdom.

Three of Swords

Key ideas: loss, unhappiness, health issues.

This is an unpleasant card that predicts loss, heartache and having to face disappointments and difficulties – and sometimes doing it alone. It can talk of a health issue, especially one involving the circulatory system or the heart, or there may be an operation that needs to be carried out.

There is one mitigating circumstance, which is that only one aspect of life should be disturbed, rather than all of it. If the situation is a really challenging one, it may even be worth the subject finding a therapist to give them coping strategies.

Extra Meanings
There may be three people in a relationship, or a relationship may go through troubled times.

Reversed
This is still a problematic card either way up, although it is not as bad when reversed. The questioner may need to visit the dentist or have some other minor procedure, or they may suffer a loss and heartache, but not a crushing kind. Tradition says that when the Three of Swords is reversed, the questioner will soon go to a funeral, and I have often found that to be true.

Astrology
Saturn in Libra.

Kabbalah
Binah, the sphere of understanding.

8: The Suit of Swords

Four of Swords

Key ideas: recovery, working as a healer.

The traditional meaning of this card is recuperating after a battle, so it means getting over an exhausting patch. However, there is a connection with hospitals, care homes, hospices, complementary therapies, and so on. Although the standard interpretation is recovery from illness, I have seen this card showing up when a client finds a job in a hospital or starts working as a healer. I have even known questioners trying to move house and finding their new home near a hospital, a care home or even a cemetery!

Extra Meanings
The questioner needs to take time out and work out how to improve their situation.

Reversed
A sick person will need time to recover or will require more treatment before healing can be assured. A stressful and challenging phase will continue, and there may also be financial losses.

Astrology
Jupiter in Libra.

Kabbalah
Chesed, the sphere of love.

The Tarot Journey in Colour

Five of Swords

Key ideas: a quarrel, walking away from something.

Fives are often difficult cards, and this one talks of quarrels or abuse that may turn violent. There is jealousy, spite and malice alongside anger and loss, which may mark a parting of the ways, and this parting may actually be a blessing in disguise. The questioner should avoid difficult situations whenever possible.

Extra Meanings
If you are working to a specific goal, you may view others as rivals who you need to defeat, though it would be much better in the long run to back off and take a less aggressive attitude.

Reversed
There are strife and arguments, but these should end soon. Tarot tradition says that the questioner might go to a funeral in the near future.

Astrology
Venus in Aquarius.

Kabbalah
Geburah, the sphere of power.

8: The Suit of Swords

Six of Swords

Key ideas: moving to a safer place, relief from poverty.

If ever a card related to those poor people trying to reach our shores by crossing the channel in rickety boats, this is it! This card is so evocative of a refugee family seeking safety and a better life that its meaning is obvious.

The questioner's life will become easier because it will be as though they are moving into quieter, safer waters and reaching a welcoming coast. There may be relief from poverty or loss and an end to sadness and loneliness. It can mean leaving a tiresome job that isn't going anywhere and doing something else. This card can indicate travel over a long distance, and the journey can bring a turning point for the better.

Extra Meanings
The questioner may need a change of outlook or attitude, or perhaps they should find better friends and colleagues. There may be a better vehicle or a change in how the client gets about.

Reversed
There may be losses due to carelessness.

Astrology
Mercury in Aquarius.

Kabbalah
Tiphareth, the sphere of beauty.

Seven of Swords

Key ideas: theft, running away.

There are two different meanings to this card. First, the questioner must be on guard against theft, fraud, or business losses due to others being dishonest, so the client may need legal or professional advice. The second meaning is that the questioner must move away from a difficult situation and start afresh. The move will exact a price, which may be financial or emotional, and something will have to be left behind, but the outcome will be a significant improvement in conditions.

Extra Meanings
A project may need to be set aside for the time being.

Reversed
There may be theft or fraud around the questioner, and the client may even suffer a break-in or find their vehicle broken into. Care needs to be taken in all spheres of life. The client will require legal or official advice of some kind soon.

Astrology
The Moon in Aquarius.

Kabbalah
Netzah, the sphere of endurance.

8: The Suit of Swords

Eight of Swords

Key idea: being unable to move.

There are a couple of meanings to this card, although they both involve restriction. On one hand, the client may be stuck in a situation that limits their ability to move or change their life for the better, which could be due to family circumstances, finances, health and so forth. On the other hand, the questioner may be so bound up in negative thinking or so tied to the past that they can't set it aside and move on.

Extra Meanings
This card can refer to actual imprisonment or being stuck indoors for a while, or heaven forbid, being stuck in lockdown again.

Reversed
Restrictions will soon end, but there may be hardship to live through before this happens. The subject may be depressed, tired, off colour or sad. Worse still, there may be losses and even deaths in the client's environment before the mist and murk finally clear away.

Astrology
Jupiter in Gemini.

Kabbalah
Hod, the sphere of majesty.

Nine of Swords

Key ideas: worry, self-fulfilling prophecy.

This card means sleepless nights and worry, although the problem may not be as bad as the questioner thinks it is. There is a potential problem of "manifestation" or of a self-fulfilling prophecy, in that worrying too much or too frequently about something can make it happen. The client needs to relax more. There may be a health problems, especially the kind that bother women

Extra Meanings
Sometimes, this tells of a parent worrying about their children or children worrying about their parents.

Someone may be slandering the questioner or telling lies about them.

Reversed
The worry and sleepless nights will soon be over.

Astrology
Mars in Gemini.

Kabbalah
Yesed, the sphere of foundation.

8: The Suit of Swords

Ten of Swords

Key ideas: cancellation, a completely new direction.

This card represents a dead loss, a situation that is no longer tenable and a collapse of plans. Anything could be affected, and anything could end, possibly due to interference or malicious damage by others. Still, it may also be due to sheer bad luck. The questioner needs to tie up loose ends, put their previous life behind them and go in a completely new direction. Courage will be needed.

Extra Meanings
As one door closes, another will open, so check out the other cards in the spread to get some inspiration.

Reversed
Things will improve, the questioner will feel more assertive, and will recover from a bad time. However, there may still be minor hitches to face. Someone may let them down. There may be trolling, nastiness or slander to deal with.

Astrology
The Sun in Gemini

Kabbalah
Malkuth, the sphere of the Kingdom.

Page of Swords

Key ideas: a word to the wise, new opportunity to come.

PAGE OF SWORDS

As a person, this would be a bright, lively youngster.

As a situation, this can mean someone is about to give the questioner good advice or warn them about looming trouble. There may even be news of bad behaviour on behalf of others. On the other hand, there may be good news about work or business and a good opportunity coming to the questioner.

Extra Meanings
I have often seen this card turn up when a contract needs to be signed or when some other legal or official document needs attention.

Reversed
A youngster may have problems or be in a difficult situation. The questioner should not believe everything others tell them, and they should avoid signing anything important. They should not behave in a way that could land them in difficulties.

Astrology
The elements of Earth and Air.

Kabbalah
There is no Kabbalistic connection for this card.

8: The Suit of Swords

Knight of Swords

Key ideas: a difficult man, swift action needed.

This Knight represents an energetic, enterprising, ambitious young man who is clever, capable and sharp-tonged. He may be attractive but he can be hurtful and aggressive.

Lots will happen, and the questioner must take swift action. They may need to consult a lawyer, doctor, financial expert or some other kind of specialist. They may have to take an unexpected journey for work, business or a family emergency.

KNIGHT OF SWORDS

Extra Meanings
If the questioner is into sports, games, or some form of racing, they will do well. If they support a squad or a team, they will be happy with their team's performance.

Reversed
An ambitious and difficult man will be around the questioner. He may be some kind of salesman or someone who travels for work. He is into sports, especially those that involve speed. As a situation, there may be arguments and difficulties. The questioner might need medical, engineering or legal advice.

Astrology
If you are into astrology, this Knight may have the sun or ascendant in Aquarius.

Kabbalah
There is no Kabbalistic connection for this card.

The Queen of Swords

Key ideas: a powerful woman, something needs fixing.

This is a strong and intelligent woman who would be a wonderful friend or just a very capable one with a cool head on her shoulders. Tradition says she is a widow or divorcee and she is likely to be tall. This Queen loves deeply, she is good with children and animals and she earns the respect of others.

Extra Meanings
As a situation, this card shows that something requires attention and that it will need to fixed.

Reversed
This woman is spiteful, unpleasant and unhelpful. She may be a professional or personal rival, and she can do the questioner much harm if she gets the chance. She may even be unhinged.

Astrology
If you are into astrology, this Queen may have the sun or ascendant in Libra.

Kabbalah
There is no Kabbalistic connection for this card.

8: The Suit of Swords

The King of Swords

Key ideas: a powerful and intelligent man.

This man has great qualities because he is intelligent and thoughtful, but he can be difficult. If the questioner needs expert advice, this man will be an excellent choice. He can be arrogant and argumentative. Oddly enough, tradition says he is sexy and a good lover, but while an affair might be passionate and exciting, living with him would not be easy.

He may be into sports as a profession or he may have spent time in the military.

Extra Meanings
The questioner will soon have to take command of a situation and appear to be strong and courageous, even if they are nervous on the inside.

KING OF SWORDS

Reversed
This is an extremely difficult and attractive man, so the questioner could find themselves involved in an upsetting affair. Frankly, it would be best to avoid getting involved with this man, however tempting he may be.

Astrology
If you are into astrology, this King may have the Sun or Ascendant in Gemini.

Kabbalah
There is no Kabbalistic connection for this card.

9: Some Simple Tarot Spreads

There are as many spreads as there are Tarot readers, but let's look at a few simple ideas for you to try out.

A Basic Spread of Seven Cards

Spread out all the cards in your deck in a row face down and ask your questioner to go along the row, picking out seven cards they feel drawn to. This kind of reading is not easy to make into a coherent story, but you can still make sense of the cards for your questioner if you use the tips I have listed below.

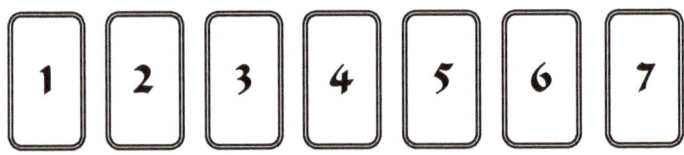

- Check to see how many Major Arcana cards are present. There should be something like two Major cards to five Minor ones. If there are more Major cards than this, something big is happening in the client's life.
- If there is only one Major card or none at all, the questioner's life is quiet at the moment, and they are in charge of their own affairs and not struggling against fate or destiny.
- Check the number of Court cards. If there is only one, this denotes an important person in the questioner's present or future.
- If there are several, the questioner may live or work among many people, none of whom are significant.
- Check the suits, including the suits the Court cards belong to. If the cards are mainly Cups, what is that telling you? Ditto if the reading is mainly Wands, Pentacles or Swords.

A Designated Spread

The idea here is the same as above, but this time, we designate the seven positions to specific issues. There are any number of ideas that you can use, but here are two to get you started:

9: Some Simple Tarot Spreads

A General Approach
The questioner.
The situation.
Past events that influence the situation.
Unhelpful people.
Helpful people.
What should the questioner do?
The future outlook for this situation.

Here is a more psychological approach:
The questioner.
What the questioner fears.
What the questioner hopes for.
What is holding the questioner back.
What will help the questioner to advance.
Surrounding circumstances.
Outcome.

Relationships on the Cards
Suppose your questioner is concerned about a love relationship. In that case, a three-card spread can be helpful as this will show how the questioner feels, while a second three-card spread will reveal how the other person feels. A more extensive spread, such as the one above, might be even more helpful.

Choosing Between Two Roads
If you have two roads to go down and don't know which one to take, do the following. Tackle the first option by putting down one card to represent the problem and then three others to highlight it. Then, do the same again for the second option. If you have three or four possibilities ahead of you, you can do three or four readings of this kind and see which one looks like the best way forward.

The Choose-it-Yourself Spread
Ask your questioner to choose six topics that are important to them at the time of the reading. This puts the onus on the questioner to state what is

on their mind rather than leaving you to work out their problems. This will only work while you are training or experimenting because paying clients don't trust professional readers who want the client to give information. The following list suggests possible topics.

List of Topic Suggestions
Marriage and partnerships.
Lovers.
Children.
Parents and family.
Health.
Property and premises.
Career.
Business.
Money.
Travel.
Holidays.
Spiritual pathway.
Sports and hobbies.
Pets.

The following is a real-life example of this kind of reading in action.

Example - Luke
Luke is a pleasant young man with a secure Royal Air Force job. He admits to having no problems in his life at present, although he has had some spells of illness over the past few years, and he still has to watch his health. He wants a steady girlfriend, although he does not feel ready for marriage. He thinks he will come out of the forces in the not-too-distant future.

As this was an experiment rather than a test of my abilities, Luke was happy to choose the six categories, and I used two cards for each category.

Categories Chosen By Luke
1. Romance.
2. Short-term career.
3. Long-term career.
4. Family (parents and sister).
5. Health.
6. Money.

9: Some Simple Tarot Spreads

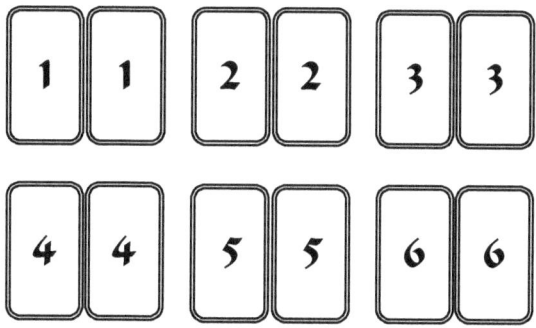

I asked Luke to shuffle and cut the cards, spread them out on the table face down and pick six pairs. I used the cards in the upright position.

The Cards
1. Five of Pentacles and Two of Wands.
2. The High Priestess and Ace of Swords.
3. Judgement and Queen of Swords.
4. The Emperor and The Hierophant.
5. Knight of Wands and Eight of Cups.
6. Four of Wands and Ten of Pentacles.

Position 1
You chose romance for your first category; the cards are the Five of Pentacles and the Two of Wands. This is a peculiar mixture because the Five of Pentacles is a sad card because it feels left out in the cold. Still, oddly enough, when applied to romance, it's not too bad a card.

The second card is the Two of Wands. Like all twos, it implies partnerships, but this will be on a social and conversational level rather than an intense, passionate level. Therefore, two or three young ladies will keep you company in the immediate future, but nothing will be heavy.

Luke replied: "I'd rather have a steady girlfriend, but obviously that's not the case yet."

Position 2
This is your short-term career situation, and here we find the High Priestess and the Ace of Swords. This implies that you may suddenly have to change gear and study something, because the Priestess implies teaching or learning. There could be a connection with engineering

through the Sword card, but I feel that things will change quickly for you, and you will have to follow your intuition about the new situation.

Luke replied: "I can't see anything new going on at the moment, but these things happen occasionally."

Position 3
We are now looking at your long-term career prospects, and you have drawn the Judgement card and the Queen of Swords, which tells me that you will not stay in the forces. The Judgement card indicates an ending with some kind of reward or bonus, and the Queen makes me think that a woman may be involved in your decision to change track. This could be the lady that you choose to marry. The severe nature of the Queen of Swords shows that whatever decisions you make will take a lot of thought.

"That seems to fit", said Luke. "I will be coming to the end of a three-year stint at around the age of thirty, so it seems to fit the picture."

Position 4
This represents your family, and you have drawn the Emperor and the Hierophant, which seem to mean your parents. The Emperor would indicate a man of authority in charge of some business venture, so I assume that refers to your Dad. The Hierophant is spiritual and also a card of tradition and marriage, so I think this represents your mother. I guess that she would be a very spiritual person and that she is very much dedicated to your father. You say you have a sister; this card would suggest that she may be getting married soon. Without pulling out further cards, I cannot tell you more about your family at the moment, but these cards are good as they imply stability.

"My father manages a shop, and until recently, my mother also had her own little shop, so they are both in business. Mother is devoted to Dad, although they always quarrel, and my sister is getting married later this year!" said Luke.

Position 5
This position represents health, and here we have the Knight of Wands and the Eight of Cups. The Eight is the crucial card as it implies that you are turning your back on the bad times of the past and moving forward to better ones. The Knight is a card of movement, so it is hard to apply it to health matters; therefore, I can only say that you will not be restricted by poor health from now on. The Knight tells you to travel about, see friends, and not worry too much. Neither of the cards indicates more trouble, but the Eight tells me you still have to be careful.

9: Some Simple Tarot Spreads

"I am much better now, but I do occasionally get twinges."

Position 6
You have chosen this position to represent money, and picked the Four of Wands and the Ten of Pentacles. On one level, it could imply that you will come into money (the Ten) through property (the Four), but on the other hand, you could invest what you have in a property. It does indicate stable finances, though, because the Four implies putting down roots, and the Ten means the start of something lasting, so these show that you will become well established financially in the future and should not be without money in years to come.

"Obviously, that's too far in the future for me to judge, but if it works out that way, I'll be very pleased", said Luke.

After the Reading
Luke asked me for more information about the girl he would likely marry, so I drew one card to see if it offered any information. As it happened, the card that emerged was the Queen of Swords.

The Long-Term Outcome
I didn't keep in touch with Luke, but I did stay in touch with his mother, so I know something of his history. He left the armed forces and opened his own business, and around that time, he met a girl, got married and started a family. The business prospered, but the marriage was difficult and eventually broke up. Luke moved to a different part of the country and found a new girlfriend, who he eventually remarried. He remained on good terms with his mother and wider family.

***

Past, Present and Future
Here is a simple idea for you to try. Allow two cards for the past, two for the present and two for the future and see what comes up, or if you prefer, you can use three cards for each period.

The Tarot Journey in Colour

The Consequences Spread
This small spread helps answer a specific question. Many ideas are based on this spread so you can adapt the spread to suit. This is one suggestion:

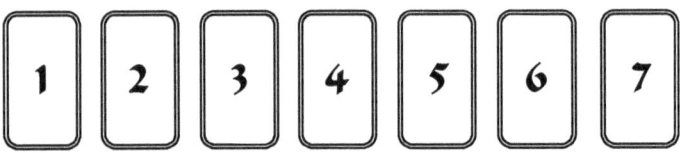

The positions:
1. The person or situation.
2. Matters affecting the person or situation.
3. The past.
4. The future.
5. Suggested course of action.
6. Outside factors.
7. Consequence or outcome.

Example - Angela
Angela is a pretty young woman of twenty whose dark eyes and masses of thick dark-brown hair give her a traveller-like appearance. She wanted a quick reading because she had just changed her job; she had not been happy in her previous job and hoped this one would be an improvement. She had taken on much responsibility with this new job and wondered if she could cope. We used my standard consequences spread and went around the pattern twice, but I used the cards just as they came out of the deck, in both the upright and reversed positions.

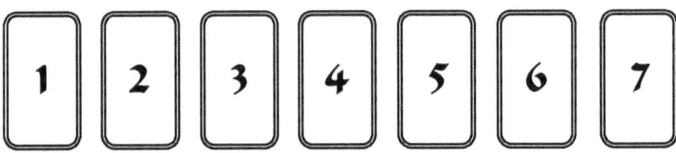

9: Some Simple Tarot Spreads

First Spread
1. Eight of Pentacles.
2. Eight of Wands.
3. Ace of Swords, reversed.
4. The Star.
5. Two of Swords.
6. The World, reversed.
7. Three of Swords, reversed.

Position 1
The first card is the Eight of Pentacles, which is truly amazing because it often turns up when the questioner changes their job! This is a good omen because it tells me that the job is definitely going to be better than your last one. Still, you will have to work hard to justify the higher status you are being given.

Position 2
Another astonishing card - this time, you have drawn the Eight of Wands, which is associated with travel. So even a complete beginner could work out that you are starting a new job which will involve some travelling for you – let alone the fact that this particular job happens to be in the travel trade. (The job was working for an airline.)

Position 3
This shows past influences, and it is the Ace of Swords reversed. I guess there were some pointless arguments at your last job and a complete failure to reach any agreement.

"Yes, that's right," agreed Angela.

Position 4
Here, we have the future influence, and you have picked just about the best card for this because it is the Star. This card represents hope, optimism and faith in the future, so you should have plenty of good things to look forward to.

Position 5
This represents your direction for the future, and here you have the Two of Swords, which is a strange card to choose for this position because it represents inaction rather than action. You are being advised to go along with whatever your new bosses want of you, not make unnecessary waves or jump to conclusions. In short, just put the new job out on the water and see how it floats. Do you understand this?

"Yes," said Angela, "I guess that means I should just go along with their ideas and see how things work out."

Position 6
This should throw some light on your future environment. The card shown here is the World. This is a good card, but it is reversed, indicating that you will not get everything you seek. Still, you should find your new world enlightening and interesting. You will have to watch out for something, though, and you may not be able to travel as much in the initial stages as you would like to.

Position 7
This refers to the outcome, and here, you have drawn a problematic card. This is the Three of Swords, and it is reversed. I don't really know what to say about this. The reversed position should imply an end to sadness and worry. Is this trying to tell us there will be trouble from some unexpected source?

After the reading
Angela told me that she had been unhappy in her last job and that her first impressions of this new job had been favourable. Eventually, Angela became a supervisor in the booking department. She was able to travel a great deal around Europe while working in this job. Interestingly, the Three of Swords turned out to be extremely prophetic because several years later, the boss of the firm had a heart attack; he became so ill that he closed the business, throwing Angela and all the rest of the staff out of work. In my experience, while the Three of Swords can relate to any loss or problem, it often foretells heart trouble.

***

The Consequences Spread Using Major Arcana Cards
I used only the Major Arcana cards in this spread, all in the upright positions.
1. The person or situation.
2. Matters affecting the person or situation.
3. The past.
4. The future.
5. Suggested course of action.
6. Outside factors.
7. Consequence.

9: Some Simple Tarot Spreads

Tina

Is an attractive lady in her mid-thirties, living with her fiancé, Andrew, a kindly man with a gentle, relaxed exterior that hides a very acute mind. Until recently, Tina ran her own fashion business, but sold it and is temporarily out of work. She is wondering where she should go from here.

1. The Chariot.
2. The Hermit.
3. The Star.
4. The Fool.
5. The Hierophant.
6. The Lovers.
7. Judgement.

Position 1

Here, we see the Chariot, which means that you need to consider several demands being made upon you. You've got home needs, Andrew's needs and your own requirements. You feel that you want to be back at work or at least to be busy because the Chariot implies doing something with a purpose. This is occasionally connected with vehicles, so this could be an important part of your future in some way – or you could be travelling soon. However, the Chariot is quite unusual in that it can sometimes be retroactive, and the observations I have just made may have more to do with your past than with future events.

Position 2

Here, we see the Hermit, which is the situation you are in now. You are at home on your own and developing the thoughtful, spiritual side of your nature. You are currently relaxing and taking a break or a retreat from life. Perhaps this is something that you need to do at this time.

Position 3

This is supposed to represent the past; you have achieved a lot because you have the Star here. You've been extremely creative in the past; you've made things work, made your life work, reached for the stars, learned a lot, studied a lot and gained a lot of insight and wisdom. You've kept a hopeful, optimistic and happy outlook on life.

Position 4
This position represents the events just ahead of you, and now we see the Fool, which represents a fresh beginning. Nothing remains the same, and you won't stay in this static position for long, either. The Fool indicates something completely new, so you will not be working in the same trade or the way you did before, and the new environment will not be familiar. You also seem to be setting off on a spiritual journey.

Position 5
This is the Hierophant, which, among other things, is a card of marriage. This reading is taking place in February, and I know you plan to marry in July. Hence, the fact that this is the fifth card in the spread and the number on the Hierophant card is also five seems to link with you getting married five months from now. There is a feeling that you could be attached to Andrew in more ways than marriage – so you could be working together somehow. This card is also about tradition and traditionally doing things, so all your dealings will be straightforward and honest.

Position 6
Another lovely card here is the Lovers. This shows that you intend to do things with Andrew and will make decisions together. Whatever you do will involve teamwork, and you won't be alone.

Position 7
The outcome of all this is shown here by the Judgement card. This is a card of reward and completion, so I feel you will be pleased to be regularising your relationship into a formal marriage and partnership. You seem to have completed a phase, and there will be a sense of reward and a clean slate that will allow you to confidently move forward into a new phase.

After the reading
We had a long chat after this reading, during which Tina told me that she was interested in doing some kind of spiritual work and that she was particularly interested in energy healing.

9: Some Simple Tarot Spreads

The Long-Term Outcome

Tina and Anthony married and were happy for a while, but the marriage didn't last, possibly because they went into a business that didn't work in the long run, which may have put a strain on the marriage. Tina eventually started another business on her own and developed an interest in spirituality.

The Pyramid

The idea here is to lay ten cards out in a pyramid shape and read the cards from the base upwards, line by line. This can work for a general reading, but it is better when looking into a particular problem. Keep an eye on the suits that turn up and the number of Major Arcana or Court cards to see which predominates – if, indeed, any of them do.

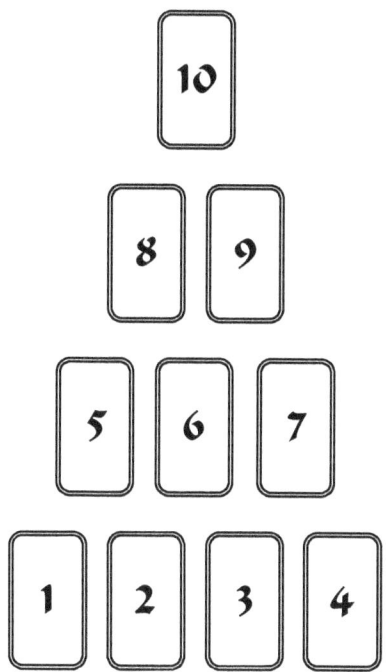

10: Complex Spreads

The Celtic Cross

The spread that many readers use is the famous Celtic Cross. I have come across several different ways of reading the Celtic Cross, and you may disagree with mine, but that's fine because you must always do your own thing where the Tarot is concerned. The best way to do this reading is with the whole deck and all the cards upright.

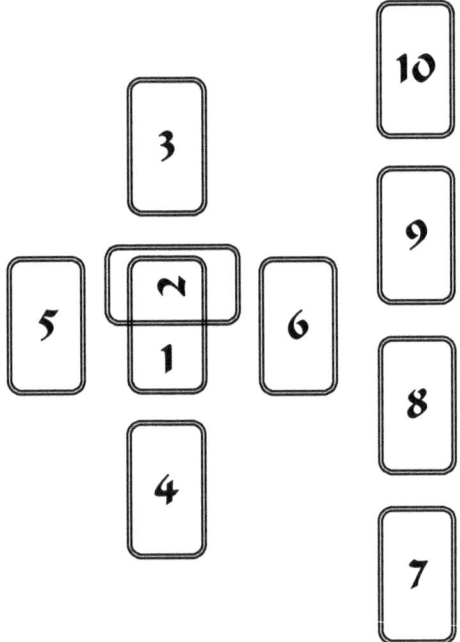

1 The problem or circumstances surrounding the questioner.
2 What they are up against.
3 The distant past.
4 The recent past, the present.
5 The near future.

10: Complex Spreads

6   The goal, aim or ambition of the questioner.
7   The questioner's feelings.
8   Outside factors.
9   The questioner's hopes and fears.
10   The outcome.

The Astrological Spread

The astrological spread is based on the twelve astrological houses, and it is popular with Tarot readers who are also into astrology. It is usual to lay twelve cards out in a circle, with the first card on the left and the rest around the circle in an anti-clockwise direction. The reader reads the cards along with the meanings of the houses. For instance, if the Ace of Wands turned up in the fourth house, it would suggest something new was about to happen in the questioner's home life.

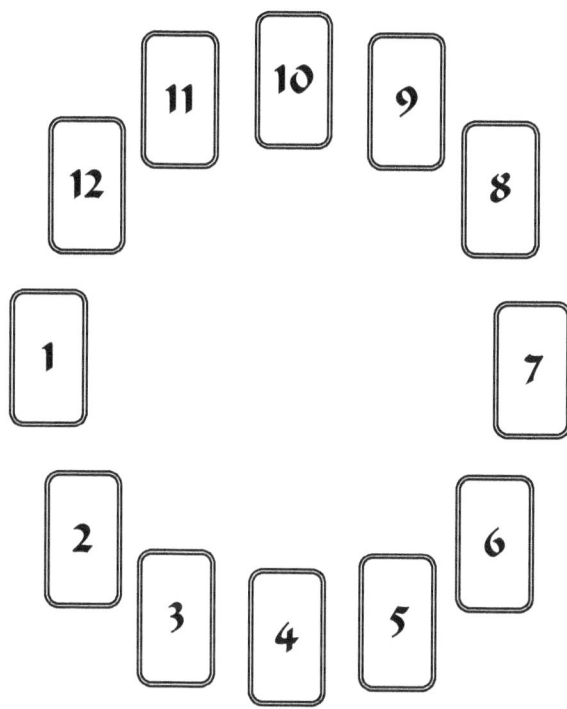

House One
This represents the questioner, their physical body, and the programming the questioner received in childhood, so it also shows the questioner's outer manner. It has some connection to health and the emotional atmosphere or circumstances surrounding the questioner during the reading.

House Two
This tells of a person's money, possessions and things the questioner values. It can also say something about the questioner's image.

House Three
This house concerns the local environment, communication, writing, business, local travel, basic education, siblings and other relatives of the questioner's own generation.

House Four
This house relates to the home, property and premises, the parents, especially mother figures, the past, instincts and any remnants of childhood behaviour or phobias. This also reflects the past, the family's background and familiar things. This can rule mother figures.

House Five
This joyful house refers to creativity, the questioner's children, holidays, fun, love affairs, glamour, show business, and even gold and jewellery.

House Six
Tradition says this is the house of servants and masters, so it rules duties, employers and employees, service to others, work, health and health-care work.

House Seven
This house is about open relationships, including working partnerships and sometimes even open enemies.

House Eight
This relates to serious matters such as shared finances, other people's resources, mortgages, taxes and corporate issues. Love, marriage and sex in committed relationships both in the sense of getting together and

splitting up. Birth and death and transformation. Even mining and things that are underground can be found here.

House Nine
This house links with expanding the questioner's horizons via travel, higher education and new environments. Also, foreigners, foreign goods and business matters relating to long-distance travel. It relates to spreading the word via publishing and broadcasting, but it is also concerned with law, important legal documents and court cases, and religious, philosophical, and mystical matters. Yet despite all this serious stuff, this house rules sports, gambling, horses, other large animals, and personal freedom.

House Ten
This is all about where what we want to become, so it concerns reputation, aims, aspirations, responsibilities, professional standing and success. It can also rule authority or father figures.

House Eleven
This house lists humanitarian ideas, group philosophies, social life, clubs and societies, friends and acquaintances, detached relationships and intellectual pursuit. Also, hopes and wishes, teaching and learning for pleasure.

House Twelve
Here we find inner thoughts, feelings, fears, self-imposed limitations, hidden resources, and abilities. Places of seclusion such as hospitals, prisons and asylums, self-destruction and addictions. Also, the psychic side of life, secrets, hidden friends and enemies. Sometimes, this concerns strategy and tactics.

The Tree of Life Spread
If you are seriously into the Kabbalah, you can lay the cards out in the Tree of Life shape and read each card in conjunction with its sephira. This concept is similar to the astrological reading, but it requires a good deal of Kabbalistic knowledge.

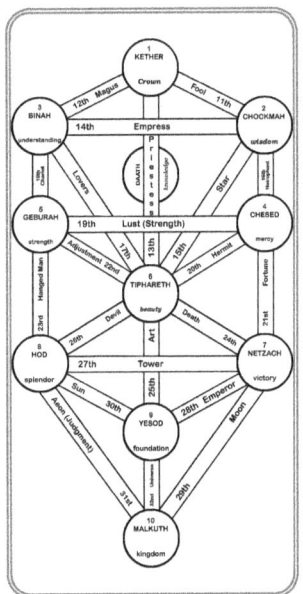

Large Spreads
There are horseshoe spreads that use many cards and spreads that lay out several rows of cards using half the deck. I find these large spreads confusing, but try them yourself and make up your own mind.

True Stories
I have mentioned this before in this book: the type of cards that turn up in a spread can give you a clue as to what is happening. The following true story shows you what I mean.

Jenny's Story
Jenny was a regular client of mine, but one day, she came for a reading and I couldn't help noticing she was very agitated. Unusually, Jenny told me the problem before I started the reading because she wanted me to focus on what was bothering her.

10: Complex Spreads

Apparently, her aged mother was going down with Alzheimer's, and the poor lady had taken her entire savings out of the bank and put them in a safe place, but the poor old dear had forgotten where her safe place was!

I was perplexed. How in heaven's name was I supposed to solve this dilemma? I asked my spiritual guides to give me a clue while I set out the cards. When I had laid the cards out, I couldn't help noticing that nearly all of them were Swords, so this had to mean something. I asked Jenny if her mum might have put the money in a place where she kept sharp metal implements – something like swords but obviously not real swords. I suggested she look in the kitchen drawers, a toolshed or the garden shed. Jenny said she would look in those places and let me know the outcome. Two weeks later, Jenny rang to tell me what had happened. She had told her husband what I had said, and despite being sceptical, he agreed to take Jenny to her mother's house and have a look. They looked around and soon found an old handbag containing the lady's savings in the garden shed, tucked in among the garden tools!

***

Aces

If an Ace appears in a small layout, it depicts a new issue, but if several Aces show up, the questioner is about to change their life in a big way. It is worth looking at the other cards in the spread to see what they say about it. The following true story shows how this works:

Linda

Linda's reading showed all four Aces, along with the Fool, the World and the Magician, all of which shrieked, "starting a new life". I told Linda she would turn away from her current life and do something completely different and that she would be very adventurous for a while. I didn't see Linda again for a few years after that, and when she returned, she reminded me of that reading and its outcome.

Linda was a nurse who had given up her job, moved out of her rented flat and gone to Africa to help needy people. She did a lot of good work there and enjoyed an exciting love affair with a doctor, but the relationship didn't last. Eventually, she tired of the scenario and returned to everyday life. She told me she was glad she had taken the risk and had such a wonderful adventure. I really admired this daring lady.

The Tarot Journey in Colour

When Something Catches Your Eye
If a particular card seems to draw your attention, it is trying to tell you something. Similarly, if a card falls out of the deck while you are shuffling, it may have something interesting to say. In short, let the cards talk to you, but also allow your intuition to guide you.

Journal Notes
While you are learning, and even afterwards, it is worth making notes of the spread and your interpretation of it; then, you can go back over your notes a few months later to see how things worked out.

11: How To Link Cards Together To Tell A Story

The problem I come across when teaching the Tarot is that students often understand the meaning of the cards individually, but they find it difficult to link cards together to extract their story. This blockage is so common that I have decided to devote a chapter to it. This will be useful to beginners as well as those who have been reading cards for a while.

Linking Two Cards
So, let us do some simple exercises linking a couple of cards to see what they tell us. We'll start with two cards that are similar or have a similar meaning among the various interpretations ascribed to each card. This will make sense when you check out the examples.

Linking Similar Cards

The Four of Pentacles   **The Nine of Cups**

   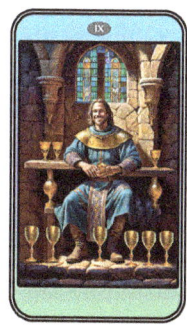

The link here is satisfaction, with the Four of Pentacles talking about having plenty of money and being a bit smug about it. At the same time, the Nine of Cups is satisfied with everything in life and may also be a bit smug. So, the reading would indicate good luck for the client, but they shouldn't allow it to go to their head.

The Tarot Journey in Colour

Here is a less obvious example, but it still works:

The Four of Wands.   **The Three of Pentacles.**

Although there are a variety of meanings attached to both these cards, the link is about putting down roots or something to do with property or premises. So, the client could be moving house, renting business premises, expanding a property, improving premises or something along those lines.

Linking Dissimilar Cards
Now, let's see what we can do with two dissimilar cards. These cards came out of the deck randomly rather than being specially chosen for this example:

The Seven of Swords.   **The Empress.**

The Seven of Swords can indicate theft or maybe a questioner who needs to escape from a bad situation. It can mean trying to make the best of a bad situation, and it can even have legal implications. The Empress means abundance, plenty of what's needed and things coming to fruition. So, what can we do with these two?

11: How to Link Cards Together to Tell A Story

The way round this one is to read the cards sequentially; for instance, by saying that after a dreadful time during which the questioner suffered losses and thefts or had taken the wrong road in life, the questioner gets their act together, resulting in a much better lifestyle filled with abundance and joy. Another way to look at this is to suggest that only by leaving a bad situation can the questioner move towards a better way of life.

Here is another tricky pair of cards taken at random:

The Hierophant.   **The Ace of Wands.**

The Hierophant can represent a kindly advisor, a traditional way of doing things, or even a religious ritual. The Ace of Wands represents a beginning, an actual or metaphorical birth or rebirth, a new concept or a new creative endeavour.

The simplest answer is that someone will advise the questioner in connection with a creative endeavour or a new pathway in life. A more off-the-wall idea is that the questioner will soon be married (tradition, religion, etc.), bringing a successful new lifestyle and possibly the birth of a child. In this case, it would be a good idea to check the surrounding cards or maybe put a few more cards down to get more clarity.

If All Else Fails
If the reading is completely meaningless, ask the client to reshuffle the cards and think about their current position while you ask your spiritual guides to give you some helpful information about the client's current status.

The Four-Card Exercise
The following ideas have come from the workshops I have done over the years, as they help the student judge a small spread of cards rather than

getting lost while dealing with too many cards at once. As I am using four cards for this exercise, the ratio suggests that there should be one Major Arcana card, one Court card and a couple of numbered cards, but anything can happen.

Here are four cards taken at random for an imaginary client:

Ten of Wands.   Knight of Wands.   Four of Swords.   Knight of Cups.

  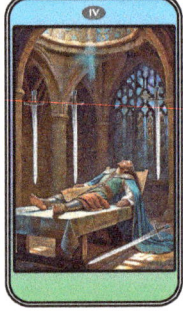 

There are no Major Arcana cards here, but there are two Court cards, both being Knights, and the presence of the two Knights catches my eye. The Knights could represent people in the questioner's life, but they may also signify that this questioner is on the move in a big way. There are two Wand cards, which say that this reading is about the questioner's daily activities and working life.

What do we make of this? The Ten of Wands represents a heavy burden, but a goal is in sight. The Four of Swords means rest and recovery after a battle, but it can mean that something is coming to a conclusion or someone is leaving the scene. The Knights suggest movement in the questioner's affairs and a significant change of surroundings. Both Wands and Swords are Yang cards, which are highly masculine in their energy, so the questioner will find the courage and assertiveness to deal with the changes ahead.

You might come up with something entirely different for this reading, but that's fine, too.

11: How to Link Cards Together to Tell A Story

Let's have another go at this idea, using another four cards taken at random from the deck:

Page of Cups.   **Three of Cups.**   **Four of Pentacles.**   **The Tower.**

This is one of those spreads that could defeat any Tarot reader, but let's see what we can make of it. Firstly, there is one Major Arcana card, the Tower, which denotes a shock, an upheaval, a nasty surprise or even a complete disaster, but there is always enlightenment to follow.

Two of the other cards are Cup cards, one being a Court card. The Page of Cups can bring messages of love or gifts or good news generally, and the Three of Cups would endorse that idea and add the feeling of a celebration to come. Another great card follows, which is the Four of Pentacles. It looks as if everything in the garden is rosy for this questioner.

However, the Tower shows a hidden problem that will come to light. Nevertheless, it may be better for the issue to come out into the open where the questioner can deal with it.

Of course, this reading can only make sense with a real-life client, especially if the questioner follows it up by telling you what is going on.

The Tarot Journey in Colour

An Example Using Seven Cards

**Six of Cups.   Wheel of Fortune. Seven of Wands. Page of Wands.
Temperance.   Ace of Cups.   Five of Cups.**

We have two Major Arcana cards, one Court card, two Wand cards and three Cup cards, suggesting emotion, feelings and moodiness are at the back of this reading.

The Reading
The first card is the Six of Cups, which shows that the questioner is looking back to a happy time in the past, but this is followed by the Wheel of Fortune, which signifies a time of change.

The Seven of Wands means that the questioner will soon have a lot on their plate, and this may even increase after a message (Page of Wands) says there is more to be done. This card may even relate to a young person whom the questioner will need to protect.

The Temperance card says that the questioner can cope with everything they will have on their plate.

11: How to Link Cards Together to Tell A Story

The Ace of Cups brings love and gifts to the questioner.

The main fly in the ointment is the last card, which shows that something or someone will prove to be a letdown.

On the whole, this is a happy reading. Still, emotions are running high, and there is a warning that not everybody will treat the questioner nicely. Once you have done a reading like this and told your questioner what you can about their situation, they will probably fill you in with what is going on in their life, after which you can go over the reading again and tell them more about their future in the light of their actual circumstances.

12: Colour And The Tarot

Those who have trained in the psychic or spiritualist tradition relate well to colour, often using colour in connection with the chakras. Some spellcasters are also into colour, using coloured candles, paper, crystals and ribbons to bring about a particular effect, such as green for money, red for passion, purple for business and pink for love. Colours mean different things to different people; we all like or dislike specific colours. In addition to this, there are astrological, religious and social connections to colours.

The colours you see on the cards will vary according to the deck you use, but if a colour stands out or predominates in a reading, it's worth noting. You can use this idea for Tarot cards and the various oracle cards that are around.

Colour and the Chakras
The seven main chakras are spiritual centres that run through the body from front to back, lining up along the spine. The system starts at the bottom, working its way upwards, and each chakra is linked to a colour.

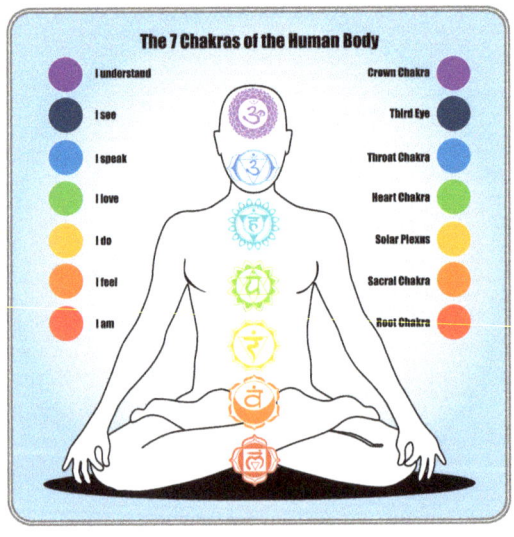

12: Colour and the Tarot

The Base Chakra

Colour: **Red**

This chakra is situated at the bottom of the spine, and it is associated with survival, so it concerns the basic needs of food, clothing and shelter. It is intuitive rather than emotional or spiritual, so if we feel uncomfortable in the company of a particular person or a specific place, it is the base chakra that is sending us a warning message. This chakra is linked to masculine sexuality but also with pregnancy and childbirth.

The base chakra refers to our time in the womb and our first six months of life. It rules our childhood experiences, early school life and early days in general. This chakra concerns the home, along with safety and seclusion, and it represents a base from which we can venture out. It also denotes the start of a journey, a new enterprise or a new phase of life. It also relates to our background, family history and reputation, and our relationship to our mothers.

The Sacral Chakra

Colour: **Orange**

The sacral chakra is in the abdomen, and the back of it connects with the lumbar spine, the sciatic nerve and the pelvis. This is an intuitive chakra rather than an intellectual or spiritual one, and it concerns emotions. It indicates connecting and sharing but also independence. It talks of joining but also separating, and it concerns shared resources and separate ones. This chakra tends to react to circumstances and things that happen to us. The sacral chakra forms between the ages of six months and two-and-a-half years, so events that occur at that time will have a profound influence on the individual.

The sacral chakra rules love, sex and important relationships. It also rules idealism and the urge to help others, but this can lead to a tendency to attract lame ducks. Fortunately, there is a sense of self-preservation that kicks in here, so the person should be able to avoid those who want to take advantage of them. The ideal situation is to give and take but not to lean too much on others or allow others to become takers.

The Solar Plexus Chakra

Colour   Yellow

The solar plexus chakra is just above the navel, and it extends through to the spine. This chakra is vital to those climbing the corporate ladder because it rules self-confidence and leadership ability. It also rules information technology and communication. It specifically rules the obtaining of information through education, reading, television and the internet. However, it also governs the ability to disseminate information in the form of teaching, presentations, blogs, articles and books. It rules curiosity and a desire to learn. Tradition says this chakra was formed between the ages of two-and-a-half and four-and-a-half, so check what happened then.

The solar plexus chakra is associated with ideas, aims and ambitions and with having the grit, determination, courage and confidence to go after these things. The sacral chakra is about leadership and the ability to direct and control others in a managerial role. However, self-control is also ruled by this chakra, along with the amount of leeway that we allow ourselves or give to others. When working well, this chakra endows the ability to make a great success in life.

The Heart Chakra

Colour   Green

This is the second of the emotional chakras, as opposed to those dealing with survival, intellectual or spiritual issues. This chakra is about love in all its forms, along with the ability to relate to others. The heart chakra is concerned with emotional security and with the certainty of being loved by others. It seeks to form a balance between the need for love and the desire for spiritual excellence, so it rules selflessness, compassion, devotion and a reasonable measure of sacrifice on behalf of others. It is said to rule unconditional love.

The heart chakra is also concerned with the good things in life, such as creativity and pleasure from art, music and dance, and it connects with craft work or creating a lovely home or garden. So, this links with physical and emotional healing on the one hand but also with fun, amusement and upliftment, in addition to relaxation, rest and recovery. It is linked with events that occurred during the ages of four-and-a-half and six-and-a-half, so it is worth looking back to your life at that age to see how it affected you.

12: Colour and the Tarot

The Throat Chakra

Colour   Light blue

The throat chakra is located at the throat at the front, through the nape of the neck at the back. This is a mental or intellectual chakra that is associated with logic, reason and common sense. This chakra is associated with learning, teaching, taking in knowledge, and communicating it to others. It can rule artistic interests, especially those that can be listened to, such as music and poetry. People with strong throat chakras take responsibility for their own actions, and they don't look around for people to blame when they make mistakes. They take credit for their own achievements and accept their own shortcomings, so they earn the respect of others. They are loyal, decent, trustworthy and honest. While also diplomatic and tactful, they aren't stupid, so they quickly see through the machinations of others.

This chakra is said to hark back to the things that happened to the person between the ages of six-and-a-half and eight-and-a-half. Some traditions see this chakra as a filter that keeps the mundane world and all its doings away from the spiritual world that is the focus of the upper chakras. It rules the ability to communicate our needs to others and to hear what they have to say to us.

The Brow Chakra
(Also known as the Third Eye Chakra)

Colour   Dark blue

This chakra is located in the middle of the forehead and is known as the third eye. This chakra rules extra-sensory perception, and it forms a bridge between the mundane world and the world of spirit. It is also associated with psychology in the sense of being able to understand ourselves and others. It brings the gifts of intuition and inspiration and the ability to access messages from the spirit world. It is primarily connected to clairvoyance and second sight. This chakra helps us to be decent, honest, loyal, reliable and sympathetic, to use our strength positively and to make the planet a better place.

This is the first of the spiritual chakras, but it also rules thinking, imagination and creativity. This chakra is also linked to memory, so it allows people to learn from past mistakes and move on to something better in the future. Tradition links this chakra to the relationship with the mother and to the person's feelings about their mother, so there is that link to the past, along with a vision of the long-term future. Another link to the past is the age group that this chakra is said to relate to, which is eight-and-a-half to ten-and-a-half.

This chakra is adept at interpreting symbols that the person receives in dreams or during spiritual work. It is linked to such things as oracle cards and the Tarot through its ability to translate images into messages. The insight that this chakra endows enables individuals to see through lies and subterfuge and to know what is going on.

The Crown Chakra

Colour   Purple

This chakra rules spirituality, brotherhood and faith. This chakra contains memories of past lives and glimpses of the next life. This is the gateway to the higher consciousness, guided intuition and an understanding of the real meaning of life and the afterlife. The Crown chakra rules faith, trust, prayer, meditation and wisdom, but it also links to happiness and joy. Feelings of fear, loneliness, isolation and grief can be linked to this chakra even when it is correctly aligned because intense suffering can lead people to search for answers and to find spirituality, and this may eventually lead them to guide, comfort and counsel others.

An Above the Body Chakra

There are many other chakras in the body, and even some that are found above the head. Here is one that is above the head that has a link to colour. It is called the eighth chakra and is associated with a strange combination of money and death.

Colours   Gold or white

Some traditions say this chakra sits immediately above the head. In contrast, others say it is sited several inches above the head. Some traditions see this as a gold orb, and others see it as a white glow or even a white flower.

Oddly enough, people ruled by this chakra are incredibly money-minded! And they may need to make or keep money or use it to give them power over others. Those who can't keep money in their pockets at all and who are always broke could benefit from having healing given to this chakra.

This chakra is said to be particularly important at the point of death, as some believe that the soul leaves the body from the crown of the head. This means the eighth chakra is the link between the mundane world and the next life and that it carries our karma with it. However, many psychics and those who work in hospitals and hospices witness souls leaving bodies through the naval, as though attached to a new umbilical cord – so I leave you to work this one out for yourself.

12: Colour and the Tarot

Colours and Astrology

The signs and planets in astrology are all linked to colour and characteristics.

Sign: **Aries.**
Planet: Mars.
Colour: Red.
Character: Sociable, courageous, fun-loving, assertive.

Sign: **Taurus.**
Planet: Venus.
Colour: Pink or green.
Character: Reliable, capable, good with money, obstinate.

Sign: **Gemini.**
Planet: Mercury.
Colour: Yellow.
Character: Curious, intelligent, friendly, determined.

Sign: **Cancer.**
Planet: The Moon.
Colour: White or silver.
Character: Good with the public, family-minded, moody.

Sign: **Leo.**
Planet: The Sun.
Colour: Orange or gold.
Character: Generous, capable, good leadership qualities, arrogant.

Sign: **Virgo.**
Planet: Mercury and possibly also Chiron.
Colour: Taupe.
Character: Intelligent, good friend, good at details, a worrier.

Sign: **Libra.**
Planet: Venus.
Colour: Pink or green.
Character: Musical, friendly, popular, indecisive.

Sign: **Scorpio.**
Planet: Pluto, but also Mars.

The Tarot Journey in Colour

Colour: Magenta.
Character: Deep thinker, intelligent, capable, hot-tempered.

Sign: **Sagittarius.**
Planet: Jupiter.
Colour: Royal blue.
Character: Lucky, courageous, kind, restless.

Sign: **Capricorn.**
Planet: Saturn.
Colour: Grey, brown, tan, mustard.
Character: Ambitious, capable, family minded, materialistic.

Sign: **Aquarius.**
Planet: Uranus, but also Saturn.
Colour: Bright blue, turquoise.
Character: Idealistic, intelligent, good friend, impractical.

Sign: **Pisces.**
Planet: Neptune but also Jupiter.
Colour: Sea-blue green.
Character: Helpful, spiritual, kind, chaotic.

Chinese Astrology

The Chinese link directions and colours to mythical figures.

North	The blue or black turtle.
East	The green dragon.
South	The red phoenix.
West	The white tiger.
The centre	The yellow-clad emperor.

12: Colour and the Tarot

Colour Oddments

Aura readers use colour when interpreting the aura.
- Some healers wrap their patients in coloured cloths when giving healing.
- If you have to attend an important event and need to stand out, take a tip from our late Queen and wear a bright colour.
- If you want to look classy, take a tip from our new queen and choose cream, white or silvery grey.
- If you want to look sophisticated (and slim), wear black.
- If you want to look spiritual or angelic, choose pastel colours.
- If you need to make money, green is the right colour.
- If you want to do business, wear purple.
- If you want confidence, power and strength, go for yellow.
- If you want to teach, wear some yellow, such as a scarf or belt.

13: Quick Clues To The Meanings Of The Cards

This gives you a quick and easy way of referring to the cards, which will be a handy addition for those of you who mainly read the cards by the images and colours on them, allied to your own intuition.

If you like keeping a journal, you can photocopy this chapter and paste it into your book for future reference.

The Major Arcana

0 The Fool
A fresh start or one that could take you in any direction. You don't have the skills or knowledge to deal with the new arrangements, but they should have a good outcome because spirit will be there to protect you.

I The Magician
A new beginning, but you have the necessary skills, so it could represent a new job, self-employment or opening a business. It would be best if you market yourself. Sometimes, this predicts an important new man coming into a questioner's life. Beware of liars and confidence tricksters.

II The High Priestess
Experience and wisdom combine with intuition, a cool head ruling a warm heart. Help, advice, tuition. Something has yet to be revealed.

III The Empress
Comfortable and beautiful surroundings. Land and gardens. A loving, motherly woman, possible pregnancy in the family. Abundance and fruitfulness and money to spend on the home and family.

IV The Emperor
The masculine force. A man of influence, maybe a father or husband or a mentor. Power and status for the questioner. Success and achievement.

13: Quick Clues to the Meanings of the Cards

V The Hierophant
Tradition and conventional behaviour. A spiritual authority, a kindly advisor who shows the questioner how to stay on the straight and narrow. Possible marriage.

VI The Lovers
Choices, possibly due to a relationship or family matter. The beginning of a relationship or the renewal of a love affair. Beauty is in the questioner's surroundings, but they need to spend money on their appearance.

VII The Chariot
Movement and change. Travel and transport. Conflict results in victory and triumph over adversity. The need to control opposing or conflicting forces.

VIII Strength
Patience, endurance, tact and diplomacy, the gentle force. Recovery from illness and better health. Return of confidence and assertiveness.

IX The Hermit
Quiet contemplation and introspection. The questioner needs to centre themselves and centre their psychic energies. Wise counsel or enlightenment. A time of retreat and reflection and of being alone by choice.

X The Wheel of Fortune
Changing circumstances, hopefully for the better.

XI Justice
Legal matters that produce a just result. Fairness, an apology given or received. Balance, harmony. Arbitration.

XII The Hanged Man
Suspension and a temporary state of limbo. Spiritual versus material concerns. Sacrifice of one thing to have another. Initiation into a new group through shared experiences of pain. Martyrdom.

XIII Death
Change, transformation. Something old gives way to something new. A situation comes to an end. Someone may die, but it is more likely that a circumstance will come to an end.

The Tarot Journey in Colour

XIV Temperance
Moderation in all things, balance in life, things working as they should. Peace, contentment and harmony.

XV The Devil
Unnecessary guilt feelings. Bondage to a situation that is no longer relevant. Misplaced loyalties. Sex, lust, addiction. A heavy commitment that is basically good, such as a mortgage or a long-winded enterprise. Envy is coming to the questioner.

XVI The Tower
A shock or a collapse of plans. An awakening that brings enlightenment. A surprise, but not necessarily a disaster. Something wrong with the place the questioner is living in.

XVII The Star
Faith in the future, making plans. Hope, success, expansion of horizons. Education. Perhaps a connection to astrology.

XVIII The Moon
Dreams, illusions, self-delusion and overwhelming emotion. Lies and mysteries. Muddled feelings and indecision. Illness maybe.

XIX The Sun
Joy, happiness, success. Trials overcome; exams passed. Children or pets might figure in the questioner's life soon.

XX Judgement
The end of a project or an assessment of its worth. Something that comes alive once again. Legal matters.

XXI The World
Full circle. Completion of a cycle. A new road is ahead. Travel and expansion of horizons.

The Minor Arcana

The Suit of Wands
Wands represent day-to-day matters, creativity, education, work, business and communication.

13: Quick Clues to the Meanings of the Cards

Ace of Wands
Good news, maybe an important letter or email. A new enterprise, business success. Perhaps the birth of a child.

Two of Wands
Partnerships and enterprises that involve at least one other person. House moves, property matters and possibly delays with this. Dealing with a proud man.

Three of Wands
A new project, new job or new beginning. Travel in connection with work, negotiations or news. Marriages and other partnerships being successful.

Four of Wands
Possible move of house or premises, although delays are likely. Putting down roots. Business matters go well.

Five of Wands
A challenge or even a friendly battle. This will require patience and courage, but the questioner will win out in the end.

Six of Wands
Victory, achievement. Legal, business and other problems will soon be solved, and agreements will be reached.

Seven of Wands
Lots to deal with, opposition, embarrassment and even health problems. The questioner must deal with things a bit at a time or become overwhelmed.

Eight of Wands
Travel, possibly to a hot country. New friends, new experiences and a widening of horizons. Negatively, things could be held up through strikes, or there may be jealousy.

Nine of Wands
Most problems are behind the questioner, but one is still ongoing. Negatively, there may be health problems or someone undermining the questioner's status.

Ten of Wands
Burdens and responsibilities are on the way, and this could be worth the effort, but it could also be a lot of work for no real reward. Care must be taken.

Page of Wands
A lively, intelligent, but scatterbrained child. An important email, letter or phone call. Beginning of a friendship or romance.

Knight of Wands
A cheerful young man who travels in connection with business. Travel for work or an important visitor from far away. Avoid confidence tricksters and liars.

Queen of Wands
This lady is highly sexed, warm-hearted and a good businesswoman. She may be too temperamental or too assertive for some tastes. Otherwise, a businesslike approach will soon be needed.

King of Wands
A good communicator who may work in teaching, sales or journalism who may be helpful in a working environment. He mixes with interesting people. He may not always be truthful.

The Suit of Cups
Cups represent emotional matters, relationship issues, creativity and family life.

Ace of Cups
The start of a friendship, a good work relationship or a love relationship. A gift, a token of love.

Two of Cups
A loving partnership, possibly engagement. Good colleagues and a happy atmosphere at work. Negatively, a parting.

Three of Cups
Joy, celebration, a wedding, good times with friends, especially female friends. It can imply relief after a parting of the ways.

13: Quick Clues to the Meanings of the Cards

Four of Cups
The questioner has much to be grateful for, but it isn't quite right, so there is an air of dissatisfaction. Can indicate new friends to come. Something good may come out of the blue.

Five of Cups
Loss and sadness, even a period of mourning. All is not lost, so the questioner will soon rebuild their life.

Six of Cups
The questioner may meet up with old friends or attend a family gathering. They may look back at their childhood and reassess it. Moving backwards to move forwards.

Seven of Cups
Muddle and confusion, with too many options to choose from. It may be better to leave significant decisions for the time being. If money is holding up romance, this will soon be put right.

Eight of Cups
Times may be bad, but the questioner will turn away from people and situations that aren't doing any good, and life will improve. Tradition says a fair-haired woman may soon be helpful.

Nine of Cups
Satisfaction and pleasure are on the way, but the questioner must guard against smugness or selfishness.

Ten of Cups
Joy, happiness and prosperity. Family life is good, but older people may find their children leaving home soon to start their own lives.

Page of Cups
A gentle, artistic, loving child or a new situation that turns out well. Education or teaching, new information, new friendships. A relationship that is fading into the past.

Knight of Cups
A kindly, friendly, romantic man who is a little weak, new friends and travel for fun or business.

The Tarot Journey in Colour

Queen of Cups
A gentle, caring, earth mother woman who is a good friend and a good home maker. Possibly a lazy woman who looks for the easy way out.

King of Cups
A kind, pleasant, friendly, warm-hearted man who is very romantic. He could be a good friend and an excellent advisor, but he may also be lazy, materialistic and a user.

The Suit of Pentacles

Pentacles represent practical matters, the things we own, earnings, business and financial matters.

Ace of Pentacles
A new source of income or a significant improvement in finances. A windfall.

Two of Pentacles
Juggling time, energy or money. Borrowing from Peter to pay Paul. It can indicate a split and people going their separate ways.

Three of Pentacles
Being given an opportunity to earn money. A move of house or improvement to property.

Four of Pentacles
Security, probably of a financial kind, but it might be some other form of security. The questioner must guard against greed and materialism.

Five of Pentacles
Fives are often challenging, and this one makes the questioner feel out in the cold. There may be financial loss or being over-extended. Looking for love in the wrong place. Being left out of things. Short-term love affairs go well, but they don't last.

Six of Pentacles
Being able to pay off debts, help others and spend money. Maybe dealing goods and money out after an ending or a separation. Giving to charity.

13: Quick Clues to the Meanings of the Cards

Seven of Pentacles
Slow growth, long-term advancement. Hard work pays off eventually, but the rewards may not be financial.

Eight of Pentacles
A new job or a promotion, work to be done. Good use of skills.

Nine of Pentacles
Money and success are on the way. Improvements to property and land. Pleasure from outdoor activities. A good clear-out before moving house.

Ten of Pentacles
Happiness, family life, success, money from achievements. Marriage, travel or other matters seem to be related to finances.

Page of Pentacles
A practical, rather introverted child, a good scholar. It could be news about finances or business.

Knight of Pentacles
A sensible, practical, dependable man who is good with business or money. Maybe miserly, though. Travel in connection with business.

Queen of Pentacles
A practical, capable and conscientious woman who fights hard for her rights. A good businesswoman but an implacable enemy. Decisions regarding business.

King of Pentacles
A good businessman who is reliable and conscientious. Can make good use of land. May be stubborn, stingy or materialistic. Good use of resources, and work will go well.

The Suit of Swords

Swords represent intellect, ideas, and mental energy but also troubles, sickness and overcoming problems.

Ace of Swords
A new idea. Power is being placed in the questioner's hands. If sick, this could indicate injections or surgery. Also engineering, work on a vehicle and work with tools.

Two of Swords
Stalemate, delay, nothing changing yet. The questioner can't see where they are going yet, so they must wait until things become clearer.

Three of Swords
Loss, separation, heartache. Illness and operations, especially regarding the heart or circulation. Dental treatment. Funerals. The start of emotional and physical recovery.

Four of Swords
Rest is needed, and this may be in order to recover from an illness or time in hospital. A retreat from fighting and a time of quiet rest.

Five of Swords
Arguments and even violence, battles and things coming to a head. Ruined plans, losses, heartbreak, spite and jealousy. A funeral is possible. The questioner needs to break away from a bad situation, and then things will improve.

Six of Swords
An important journey, maybe overseas or a visitor from afar. Delays are possible, but the questioner will soon move away from troubles into smoother waters.

Seven of Swords
The questioner may need to move on and leave some part of their life behind or get rid of a bad influence. Legal matters or insurance advice may be required. Beware of theft or a rip-off.

Eight of Swords
Being stuck in a difficult situation for a while, possibly due to family matters or heavy responsibilities. The questioner will eventually move away from restrictions. Someone may be in jail.

Nine of Swords
Sleepless nights and worry, sometimes being on the end of jealousy and slander. Women may suffer from female health problems.

Ten of Swords
Treachery, a stab in the back. A total ending of a situation, a collapse of plans. Injections and medical investigations.

13: Quick Clues to the Meanings of the Cards

Page of Swords
A clever child who is either serious or aggressive. Contracts and news about business matters. Someone keeping the questioner informed of things happening behind their back.

Knight of Swords
A clever, ambitious man or an aggressive one. There may be dealings with legal, financial, medical and other professional people.

Queen of Swords
A clever and competent woman who is cool and collected – or really vile. Legal and professional people may be needed soon.

King of Swords
A clever, serious and intellectual man whose judgement is sound, or a bully or a big-head who is impossible to live with or work with.

14: Tarot And Numbers

The numbers of the Minor Arcana cards tell a story on their own account.

- Aces stand for new issues.
- Twos are about partnerships.
- Threes talk about creativity and success.
- Fours refer to stability.
- Fives bring trouble and uncertainty.
- Sixes relate to overcoming difficulties and winning out.
- Sevens are unsettled cards with an uncertain outcome.
- Eights relate to hard work and worry, but they usually work out well.
- Nines are satisfactory.
- Tens represent the best or the worst that can happen.

Numerology and the Tarot

Numerology is easier than astrology, but you still need some knowledge to use it properly. In this book, I use the simplest form of numerology, which takes the numbers from one to nine, as this works best when combining numerology with the Tarot.

14: Tarot and Numbers

A Brief Description of Numbers

Number One
One is the number of achievements, activity, power and leadership. It is a strong number, and it is about the self. This can register success but also a lack of patience.

Number Two
This number is about partnerships, relationships, and the search for harmony at home and work.

Number Three
This represents creative enterprise and growth, and material benefits on the way. This number has a touch of showbiz, so it links to music and entertaining.

Number Four
This signifies the foundation that a person can build upon, so it talks of balance, stability and security, but it also symbolises restrictions and limitations.

Number Five
This suggests a need to break out of the enclosed structure, be active, and avoid routine and restriction. This number often points to upsetting or irritating situations and a need to break away from something.

Number Six
This number is associated with the home, family life and the past. It represents responsibility for others as well as work in general.

Number Seven
This number represents the need for rest, relaxation, and time to think and ponder because, after a while, the thoughts take shape and something useful will emerge. This number is linked to spiritual growth.

Number Eight
This number suggests achievement, financial and career success, spiritual attainment, progress, and the acceptance of responsibility.

Number Nine
A particular point has been reached, although there are always higher levels to aspire to. The soul is old, but there is always something more to learn. This is linked to education and to exploring ideas and spirituality.

Other Numbers
A few other numbers are used in numerology, but this is enough for our needs.

Spreads
Draw nine cards and link each to a number to see what the combination of the cards and the numbers means. For instance, an Ace of Swords could mean an important partnership to come if it was in position No. 2. However, it would represent a growth of spirituality and psychic development if in position No. 7.

Adding Three Cards Together
Lay out three cards and add their numbers together. Here is an example using an imaginary person who is interested in meeting someone nice:

> The Lovers.
> The Wheel of Fortune.
> The Four of Cups.

We are only interested in the number on each card rather than the images or meanings, so we add six for the Lovers, ten for the Wheel of Fortune and four for the Four of Cups. Adding these together, we get:

$6 + 10 + 4 = 20$

When we reduce the 20 down to a number between 1 and 9, we get the following:

$2 + 0 = 2$

The reading comes to number 2, which suggests a happy and harmonious relationship is on the way, which would be a good omen for the future.

14: Tarot and Numbers

Numerical Clues

If you see several cards with the same number on them in a reading, it can give your intuition a nudge; for instance, if you saw three or four cards with the number seven on them, that might tell you that something will happen in seven months, or it could indicate that a door with the number seven on it is about to become important to the client.

It is worth keeping your eyes open for anything that forms a pattern or makes your intuition kick in.

15: Tarot And The Decans

This is an ancient idea that I have resurrected for those who would find it interesting. The concept will appeal to those with a working knowledge of astrology because it is based on the decans in astrology, but it isn't difficult for a non-astrologer to understand.

NB: Some astrologers call decans decanates.

Here are the sun sign dates:

Sun Sign	Dates
Aries	March 21 - April 19
Taurus	April 20 - May 20
Gemini	May 21 - June 21
Cancer	June 22 - July 22
Leo	July 23 – August 22
Virgo	August 23 – September 22
Libra	September 23 – October 22
Scorpio	October 23 – November 21
Sagittarius	November 22 – December 21
Capricorn	December 22 – January 20
Aquarius	January 21 – February 18
Pisces	February 19 – March 20

Just as in the Tarot, there are four elements in astrology: Fire, Earth, Air and Water, and each sign of the zodiac is ruled by an element. As you will see, the system repeats itself three times to cover all twelve signs.

Aries	Fire.
Taurus	Earth.
Gemini	Air.
Cancer	Water.
Leo	Fire
Virgo	Earth
Libra	Air

15: Tarot and the Decans

Scorpio	Water
Sagittarius	Fire
Capricorn	Earth
Aquarius	Air
Pisces	Water

A Rough Guide to the System

This is the method in action for the sign of Aries:

March 21st	The start of the first decan.
April 1st	The start of the second decan.
April 10th	The start of the third decan.

The Scientific Method

There is a scientific way of doing this, and this is how it works. Each sign of the zodiac contains thirty degrees, starting at 0 deg. and ending at 29 deg. of the sign, and this breaks down into the three decans.

First decan:	From 0 deg. to 9 deg.
Second decan:	From 10 deg. to 19 deg.
Third decan:	From 20 deg. to 29 deg.

So, let's analyse the situation for the sign of Libra, which is an air sign.

- The first decan is Libra, which is sub-ruled by Libra.
- The second decan is Libra, sub-ruled by Aquarius, which is the next air sign when going round the system.
- The third decan is Libra, sub-ruled by Gemini, which is the last air sign when going round the system.

The Tarot Journey in Colour

If you are an astrologer and you have decent astrological software, you can quickly work out which decan your Sun, Moon and ascendant occupy and perhaps other planets as well. Here are all the decans and their rulerships.

The Decans

Aries – Fire
First decan: Aries sub-ruled by Aries
Second decan: Aries sub-ruled by Leo
Third decan: Aries sub-ruled by Sagittarius

Taurus – Earth
First decan: Taurus sub-ruled by Taurus
Second decan: Taurus sub-ruled by Virgo
Third decan: Taurus sub-ruled by Capricorn

Gemini – Air
First decan: Gemini sub-ruled by Gemini
Second decan: Gemini sub-ruled by Libra
Third decan: Gemini sub-ruled by Aquarius

Cancer - Water
First decan: Cancer sub-ruled by Cancer
Second decan: Cancer sub-ruled by Scorpio
Third decan: Cancer sub-ruled by Pisces

Leo – Fire
First decan: Leo sub-ruled by Leo
Second decan: Leo sub-ruled by Sagittarius
Third decan: Leo sub-ruled by Aries

Virgo - Earth
First decan: Virgo sub-ruled by Virgo
Second decan: Virgo sub-ruled by Capricorn
Third decan: Virgo sub-ruled by Taurus

Libra – Air
First decan: Libra sub-ruled by Libra
Second decan: Libra sub-ruled by Aquarius
Third decan: Libra sub-ruled by Gemini

15: Tarot and the Decans

Scorpio – Water
First decan: Scorpio sub-ruled by Scorpio
Second decan: Scorpio sub-ruled by Pisces
Third decan: Scorpio sub-ruled by Cancer

Sagittarius – Fire
First decan: Sagittarius sub-ruled by Sagittarius
Second decan: Sagittarius sub-ruled by Aries
Third decan: Sagittarius sub-ruled by Leo

Capricorn – Earth
First decan: Capricorn sub-ruled by Capricorn
Second decan: Capricorn sub-ruled by Taurus
Third decan: Capricorn sub-ruled by Virgo

Aquarius - Air
First decan: Aquarius sub-ruled by Aquarius
Second decan: Aquarius sub-ruled by Gemini
Third decan: Aquarius sub-ruled by Libra

Pisces – Water
First decan: Pisces sub-ruled by Pisces
Second decan: Pisces sub-ruled by Cancer
Third decan: Pisces sub-ruled by Scorpio

The Tarot Journey in Colour

The Decans and the Tarot
Now let's link the decans to the Minor Arcana of the Tarot.

Aries	Aries	2 Wands
Aries	Leo	3 Wands
Aries	Sagittarius	4 Wands
Taurus	Taurus	2 Pentacles
Taurus	Virgo	3 Pentacles
Taurus	Capricorn	4 Pentacles
Gemini	Gemini	2 Swords
Gemini	Libra	3 Swords
Gemini	Aquarius	4 Swords
Cancer	Cancer	2 Cups
Cancer	Scorpio	3 Cups
Cancer	Pisces	4 Cups
Leo	Leo	5 Wands
Leo	Sagittarius	6 Wands
Leo	Aries	7 Wands
Virgo	Virgo	5 Pentacles
Virgo	Capricorn	6 Pentacles
Virgo	Taurus	7 Pentacles
Libra	Libra	5 Swords
Libra	Aquarius	6 Swords
Libra	Gemini	7 Swords
Scorpio	Scorpio	5 Cups
Scorpio	Pisces	6 Cups
Scorpio	Cancer	7 Cups
Sagittarius	Sagittarius	8 Wands
Sagittarius	Aries	9 Wands
Sagittarius	Leo	10 Wands
Capricorn	Capricorn	8 Pentacles
Capricorn	Taurus	9 Pentacles

15: Tarot and the Decans

Capricorn	Virgo	10 Pentacles

Aquarius	Aquarius	8 Swords
Aquarius	Gemini	9 Swords
Aquarius	Libra	10 Swords

Pisces	Pisces	8 Cups
Pisces	Cancer	9 Cups
Pisces	Scorpio	10 Cups

Examples

I chose three celebrities at random for this demonstration.

Charles Bronson

The late star of the Magnificent Seven and the Death Wish series, sometimes called "Stoneface".

Sun:	10 deg. Scorpio	Third decan, Scorpio / Cancer
Moon:	25 deg. Sagittarius	Third decan, Sagittarius / Leo
Asc.:	1 Capricorn	Second decan, Capricorn / Taurus

Harrison Ford

He came to our notice as the sexy Han Solo in Star Wars and has wowed us in many other films.

Sun:	20 Cancer	Third decan, Cancer / Pisces
Moon:	22 Cancer	Third decan, Cancer / Pisces
Asc.:	2 Libra	Second decan, Libra / Aquarius

Joanna Lumley

Much loved British actress, star of Absolutely Fabulous, among many other things.

Sun:	10 Taurus	Third decan, Taurus / Capricorn
Moon:	11 Taurus	Third decan, Taurus / Capricorn
Asc.:	2 Scorpio	Second decan, Scorpio / Pisces

The Tarot Journey in Colour

So, now let us see which Tarot cards link with our superstars' Suns, Moons and Ascendants.

Charles Bronson
Sun sign, Scorpio / Cancer:	7 Cups	(Many options)
Moon sign, Sagittarius / Leo:	10 Wands	(Very hard work)
Ascendant, Capricorn / Taurus:	9 Pentacles	(Great wealth)

Harrison Ford
Sun sign, Cancer / Pisces:	4 Cups	(Partial happiness)
Moon sign: Cancer / Pisces:	4 Cups	(Partial happiness)
Ascendant, Libra / Aquarius:	6 Swords	(Travels to a better life)

Joanna Lumley
Sun sign, Taurus / Capricorn:	4 Pentacles	(Fairly secure)
Moon sign, Taurus / Capricorn:	4 Pentacles	(Fairly secure)
Ascendant, Scorpio / Pisces:	6 Cups	(Influenced by her roots)

16: A Couple Of Readings In Action

These two readings happened many years ago. The first is a standard reading about a man and his business, but the second still makes me giggle, as you will see when you read about it.

Mike's Business

Mike is an attractive man with wavy grey hair and a lovely smile. He seems content with his life at the moment, telling me he is happily married with two children who are still living at home. He is in business with a partner, and he and the partner can see a time in the distant future when they might want to sell up and do something more restful with their lives. As Mike didn't appear to have any pressing problems, we decided to look at the possibility of future changes in the business aspect of his life.

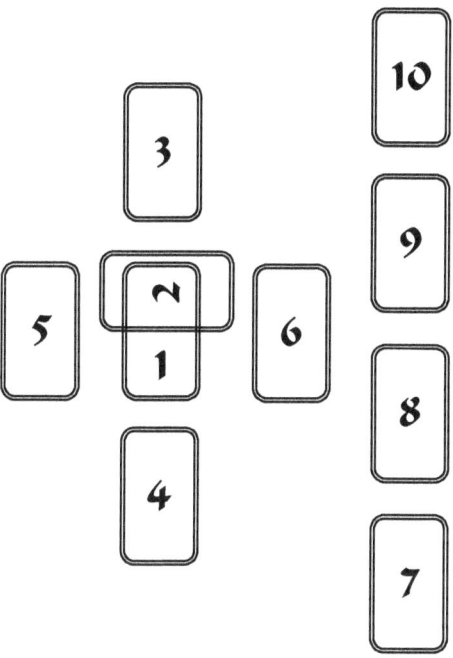

The Tarot Journey in Colour

I used only the Major Arcana, so I didn't use a significator with this spread.

1. The Hierophant.
2. Death.
3. Judgement, reversed.
4. Wheel of Fortune, reversed.
5. The Fool, reversed.
6. The Emperor.
7. The Sun, reversed.
8. The High Priestess reversed.
9. The Lovers, reversed.
10. The Devil.
11. The Reading

Position 1

The first card is the Hierophant. This card has a religious look, but its symbolic meaning is much nearer to the idea of tradition. It shows me that your life is stable and similar to the lives of other people around you. You are a traditional family man with old-fashioned values of honesty and decency that spill over into your business dealings.

Position 2

The second card is the Death card, which shows something will come to a complete end so that a new beginning can occur. The Death card does not mean that you are about to die, but it suggests that your current business situation will end and that you will have to think something through very thoroughly.

Position 3

The third position shows the distant past, and here you have the Judgement card reversed. The reversed condition of the card indicates that there has been some event or situation in the past that you don't want to see recurring. As this reading is specifically related to business, this indicates poor judgement in the past, decisions and choices that didn't work out well, and possibly even legal business-related troubles. You have suffered losses before and obviously don't wish to do so again. The Hierophant tells me that you are not a gambler by nature, so there is no reason to assume that bad judgement and losses will happen again in the future, but it is obviously something you fear, or it wouldn't have shown up in the reading.

16: A Couple of Readings In Action

Position 4
This represents the present and recent past; the card is the Wheel of Fortune reversed. I don't see the Wheel as being too bad either way up, but it tells me that circumstances regarding your work at present are not easy. All businesses have been through a recession in recent years, and you may feel tired from all the effort you put in. My feeling here is that the Wheel is turning somewhere just out of sight, which leads me to believe that things are going on in other people's heads that could profoundly affect your life in the future.

Position 5
This position denotes your immediate future, and here, the Fool is setting out on a new path and taking an unfamiliar route. Applying the card to your career shows that you prefer to stay in your present situation rather than go out on a limb with something new. This card in the reversed position sometimes indicates a kind of mental paralysis, so even though you will be shown opportunities, you will doubt your ability to grasp them and make them work. Ultimately, though, you will be compelled to make a complete change.

Position 6
This position shows the direction you should be aiming for. The card here is the Emperor, which strongly emphasises material achievement and independence.

Position 7
This is supposed to be how you see your environment now or in the future, and here you have the Sun card reversed. This card is good either way up, but the beneficial aspects of the card are weakened when it is reversed. If it were the right way up, you would have a very optimistic outlook on the future, but even with the reversal, you can be reasonably optimistic. I find that this card often has something to do with children, so you might hope that your son will take over your business or join you somehow. However, this reversed card seems to be against that happening.

Position 8
The next card is odd because it is the Priestess, and it is also reversed, this time in the position that refers to environmental factors. This could mean that you go into a new environment, and the reversed Fool ahead of you shows the possibility of making a mistake. The Priestess suggests that there are secrets that have yet to be revealed.

The Tarot Journey in Colour

Position 9
Inner emotions, hopes and fears are next, and here we have the Lovers card reversed. This shows me quite clearly that you wouldn't want to go into a partnership again because the Lovers card so often implies partnership matters. I strongly feel that even though you have plenty of moral support from the family (the Hierophant would suggest that), you will not actively work in close conjunction with any of them.

Position 10
Here, we see the Devil, which shows that something is wrong, but the Priestess tells us that you don't know what this is yet. It would be best to look into things before committing yourself to anything. There is another way of looking at part of this reading, though. The Lovers card tells me you are unhappy with your present partnership. Also, decisions that should be made jointly have been taken by others without consulting with you.

The Long-Term Outcome
The events depicted in this reading happened decades ago, and everyone involved has long since died, so I can talk about it openly now. It transpired that Mike's partner, Keith, had an affair with his wife's best friend, which caused an expensive divorce. Keith decided to sell his share of the business, and with the help of a dishonest accountant, he got Mike to buy him out at double what the business was worth. This led to the business collapse and Mike being thrown out of work. Mike soon found a job and kept his private pension scheme going, so he eventually retired in a reasonable position, albeit not the one he should have had.

The two cards that had the most to say about these events were the reversed Priestess, which showed that Keith was hiding his intentions, and the Devil, which in this case represented sheer devilry on Keith's part linked to sex and dishonesty, which led to him swindling Mike.

***

A Very Unusual Reading
This really happened and I still laugh about it all these years later. It shows that, while Tarot reading is not always easy, it does tell the truth, often with amazing clarity.

16: A Couple of Readings In Action

The Story as It Happened
I experimented by stringing a few cards together in a line and asking several other readers to interpret them. I used the British Astrological and Psychic Society committee to do the reading. If anyone should know how to read the Tarot, it is them. We chose one person to act as questioner while several of us interpreted the cards that came up for her, and it so happened that the reading was almost impossible to interpret – but was it?

The Professionals
Renée Hindle *(since deceased)* agreed to act as volunteer because Renée was a medium, psychic and rune reader, but she didn't actually read Tarot cards herself. Our six Tarot readers were Eve Bingham, Dave Bingham, Gordon Smith, Myra Russell and Fred Curtis.

Renée was a tall, slim lady who looked far more like the brilliant statistician that she was than anyone's idea of a medium. She used her mathematical talents in her work but had also been involved with clairvoyant work for many years. Renée was a widow with two grown-up children who often popped in for a chat, and they were very close to her. She also made wonderful cakes.

Renée shuffled the cards, placed them face downwards on the table, and randomly picked out six cards. The Major and Minor Arcana cards were used for the reading, although, as it happened, only Minor Arcana cards turned up. We used the cards in the upright position.

> Page of Cups.
> Page of Swords.
> Knight of Cups.
> Page of Wands.
> Eight of Wands.
> Nine of Wands.

Dave Bingham was the first to comment, telling us that Renée had picked a dreadful bunch of cards and asking if she could choose another group. Eve told him he was a coward and that a reader of his age and experience should be able to read anything. Dave then suggested that Eve start the interpretation.

While I furiously scribbled on a notepad, Eve started her reading.

Eve's Interpretation
"I can see the children here, still close to you this year. The Page of Cups would also indicate that you yourself are female, Renée."

"I'm glad you told me that," said Renée drily.

"You seem indecisive about going on holiday this year, Renée."

"That's true," she agreed, "I would love to go away, but I have too many other commitments at the moment."

"Well, Renée, I'm sure you will go away somewhere this year, as shown by the Eight of Wands and the Knight of Cups. Knights indicate movement, and I see this one showing travel. There seems to be some kind of hesitation, though – as though you will find it hard to decide. Even though you are over-committed financially and very busy right now, I'm sure travel will be important somehow."

You will notice that Eve did not read the cards in strict order, but mentally rearranged them into groups representing connected ideas. The other readers also grouped the cards into connected ideas.

Dave's Reading

"This layout is terrible; there's no guts to it, there are no problems to get your teeth into."

Eve glanced at him impatiently, "Get on with it, Dave!" she snapped.

"Well, I can see that Renée will have things to sort out this year, but there is nothing she can't handle. The Pages of Cups and Swords could certainly mean children, but there seem to be new emotional beginnings, as shown by the Knight of Cups. Renée, you're definitely going to travel in the late summer or early autumn."

"How do you get the timing on this, Dave?" I asked.

"The Eight of Wands could denote August because it's the eighth month, and the Nine of Wands could apply to September. There does seem to be a change at work following this holiday and perhaps a complete change of direction. This would be shown by the Page of Wands, which is often related to news, plus the Nine of Wands, which shows you being in command of a situation but weirdly also being hemmed in and not free to move. The other cards, the Eight and the Knight show freedom - or at least the need for freedom - so the structure of your job could be changing in some way."

Gordon's Suggestions

"Yes, I also felt it was something about work. There seems to be a reasonably happy situation before and after the changes. I'm sure you will face changes, but there's no doubt it can be sorted out".

Myra's Suggestions

"The Nine seems to show structure and organisation that will materialise from a completely new venture. However, the Page of Wands that follows

16: A Couple of Readings In Action

the Knight of Cups seems to show feelings of confusion and "Have I done the right thing?"

Fred's Suggestions
"The Pages seem to show that you are young at heart at the moment and would probably welcome a new venture. There is definitely movement forward shown by the Knight of Cups, and it seems to be in the right direction. There is skill shown in the Page of Swords but with support behind it, as shown by the Nine of Wands. There could be new ideas (Swords) of a creative nature (Wands) but also emotionally pleasing (Cups)."

Dave agreed that this could well be creative and fulfilling.

Eve suggested that the Nine of Wands shows that most of Renée's obstacles were behind her.

The Long-Term Outcome
Looking back on the reading, it comprised three Pages, one Knight and two other Wand cards; it made little or no sense at the time, which is why we all struggled with it, but the Tarot was actually telling us the truth – if we could but see it.

Page of Cups.
Page of Swords.
Knight of Cups.
Page of Wands.
Eight of Wands.
Nine of Wands.

What Happened
Renée retired from her long-term job and looked around for something to occupy her time, so she joined a voluntary organisation that collected unwanted toys, which they cleaned, mended and wrapped in pretty paper. The toys became Christmas gifts for sick children or those from impoverished families. All this happened during the summer and autumn of that year.

The three Pages represented both the children and the toys, while the Knight and the Wand cards showed movement – which, in this case, meant gathering the toys together and delivering them to the children. The job obviously meant working with others and expanding Renée's horizons, all of which was shown by the Pages, Knights and the Eight of Wands.

Renée loved her new "job", and the children she and her colleagues helped must have been delighted with their Christmas gifts.

17: Spell Casting

If you are into spellcasting and want to use the Tarot to make things happen, you need to create an altar and do something to protect your aura and your altar before you can proceed with your spell. There are as many ways of doing this as there are people who cast spells.

The following is an easy way of creating and protecting an altar, which you can do indoors or outside.

Location
Find a place in which to set up your altar where you can guarantee being left in peace for a few hours. It might be easier to find a quiet spot out of doors, as long as the neighbours can't see what you are doing.

The Elements
The elements in witchcraft are Fire, Earth, Air, Water and Spirit.

The Element of Fire
Use a tealight candle for Fire, but choose the colour of your candle to represent whatever you are trying to bring about, such as green for money, red for passion, blue for communication, pink for love or a lovely holiday, orange to get a bully off your back and so on. Put the candle into a small dish so that it won't cause a real fire.

The Element of Earth
Put a little bowl or an eggcup holding a favourite crystal on the altar to represent the Earth element. Using the right kind of crystal can help the spell to work, for instance, a piece of rose quartz for love, citrine for money or a piece of obsidian for protection. If protection is a major issue in your life, it is worth adding a second eggcup with a bit of salt in it.

The Element of Air
An incense stick, an incense burner or something of the kind will do for this. The choice of perfume is up to you, so either choose something you like or find the meaning of aromas in a book on essential oils and choose one for the outcome that you are trying to create.

17: Spell Casting

The Element of Water
A small bowl or an egg cup with a bit of spring water in it.

The Element of Spirit
You can use an image of a pentacle, which in itself represents the four elements along with Spirit, or you can use a statuette of a Buddha, an angel or anything that helps you link with Spirit. If this isn't your scene, use a bit of amethyst, as this also creates a link with Spirit.

Writing Your Spell
Take a small piece of paper – coloured paper if you like – and write down precisely what you want to happen. If you have a talent for writing verse, you can make this into a rhyme, but otherwise just jot down what you want to achieve. You may wish to end by writing, "So mote it be". Put this on the altar.

Adding a Tarot Card or Two
When you set out to make a spell, select a card or cards that represent the outcome that you wish to bring about. For instance, if you need a better boss, use the Emperor, the High Priestess, the Hierophant or maybe one of the Court cards to represent what you are hoping for.

If you have a number of things you want to manifest but don't want to go to the trouble of setting up an altar, put out a selection of cards to represent what you need, light a tealight candle, mentally ask for the outcome that you want, and leave the cards in place while the candle burns down.

Protection
Some people use an athame (pronounced ath-aim) for this. The athame is a knife that you keep specially for this work, but others prefer to use a wand, which is also kept solely for this work. Point your athame or wand all around the outside of the altar, as well as your own aura and the area in which you are spellcasting, and ask for help and protection from spirit.

You either need to know which way your room is facing or use a compass for the next bit. You need to point your athame or wand to the north and then circle around clockwise to the east, south, west and back to the north. Ask for protection for yourself, for your spell, and for anyone else you need to take care of while doing this. If you feel the need for extra help, do this more than once.

The Tarot Journey in Colour

Procedure

Light your candle (a gas firelighter is suitable for this). Pick up your written spell and read it out three times. If you are in a bad place with your life and really need the spell to work, read it out nine times (three times three).

Put the spell on the altar and leave the candle to burn down, keeping an occasional eye on it for safety.

When the candle has died off, put your paper with the spell on it in the sink and use the gas lighter to burn it, then wash the ash away. This will send the spell on its way. If you are outdoors, burn your paper spell carefully and scatter the ash on the earth.

The Moon, Days and Time

You may want to cast your spell on a particular moon phase. The only time that really won't work is the dark of the moon, which occurs just before a new moon.

A new moon is good for new projects, a waxing (growing) moon is beneficial for things that need to increase, and a full moon is excellent when you need a significant impact. A waning (shrinking) moon is useful when you need to improve a health problem. A really old moon is handy for cutting ties, ditching self-blame or getting away from hurtful people, dumping unnecessary chores and so on.

If you are into astrology, you may want to choose a day when there are good aspects to your own planets if that idea appeals to you.

Days relate to the planets, and these are the day and planet connections:

Monday:	The Moon.
Tuesday:	Mars.
Wednesday:	Mercury.
Thursday:	Jupiter.
Friday:	Venus.
Saturday:	Saturn.
Sunday:	The Sun.

17: Spell Casting

This old poem will help you see how this works.

> Monday's child is fair of face.
> Tuesday's child is full of grace.
> Wednesday's child is full of woe.
> Thursday's child has far to go.
> Friday's child is loving and giving.
> Saturday's child works hard for a living.
> The child that is born on the Sabbath day is bonnie, and blithe, and good and gay.

NB: The word "gay" in this old poem means being happy rather than being gay as we know it today – although there is no reason why one can't be gay and gay, if you see what I mean.

18: Journalling

The journal fad started with a best-selling recipe book that was followed by an attractive notebook designed for the student cook to write down their recipes and experiences. This sold so well that it took the publisher by surprise. Other publishers jumped on the bandwagon, and journals started to appear in a number of subjects, including the mind, body, and spirit genres.

There is a precedent in the world of Wicca and Witchcraft in the shape of the "Book of Shadows", which is where Wiccans and Witches note down spells and rituals, make notes of the time of the year in which they are working, draw pictures and stick in bits and pieces, and much more. Now you can buy readymade Books of Shadows, along with journals for chakras, crystals and more. The fad is wearing off, though, due to disappointing sales because most people want to spend their money on a book that gives them information, not pretty pages that they are expected to fill in for themselves. However, when it comes to the Tarot, the journal idea is not a bad one, so with this in mind, I have included a few journal-style ideas here for you to try out.

I learned to read the Tarot in the 1970s, long before anybody thought about journalling and decades before I heard of Books of Shadows. Still, my instinct drove me to make notes while practising the Tarot, and this helped me gain confidence in the cards.

How to Proceed
This couldn't be easier, as you will see from the list below:

- Find a smallish notebook that is as plain or as fancy as you like and open it to your first page.
- Note down who you are reading for.
- Write the date of the reading.

18: Journalling

- Mention if you are trying out a new way of shuffling and laying out the cards, such as cutting them into two or three piles, using reversed as well as upright cards or anything else you are experimenting with.
- Write down the name of the spread you are using, or do a little drawing to show what it looks like.
- Now, list the cards that you use, saying what you think they are telling you.

The following is an example in action.
This is January 31, 2024. I am doing a simple six-card layout for a friend called Carol, who wants me to take a look at her life at this moment in time. I have assigned a meaning to each card position so that we can see how each area of Carol's life is going at the time of the reading. I will attach two cards to each position.

Position One – Health
The Three of Wands and The Seven of Pentacles
   Brief meaning: The Three of Wands suggests that new ideas are being launched, but the amount of work Carol is doing is tiring her out, and this could have an adverse effect on Carol's health.

Position Two – Finances
The Page of Swords and The Nine of Wands
   Brief meaning: Something needs to be done which suggests that financial matters need to be addressed, although there may be a new contract soon that will bring in more money. Most problems can be solved, but one is proving difficult and can't be ignored.

Position Three – Business
The Queen of Wands and The Moon
   Brief meaning: Carol is usually represented by this Queen, so it shows that any business ideas will come from her. Nobody can see how these ideas will work out as clouds and mist surround her business at the moment. In this case, it would be a good idea to do another reading after a week or so to look into this situation.

Position Four – Family
The Eight of Wands and The Ten of Cups
   Brief meaning: Someone is on the move, and this will be followed by happiness and joy, and maybe news of a new baby in the family.

Position Five – Home
The Queen of Cups and The Ace of Pentacles

Brief meaning: A woman will help Carol, and this will lead to a new source of money coming into the home or a new form of income generated by work that she does at home.

Position Six – Travel
The Six of Pentacles and The Fool

Brief meaning: I would see this reading as telling us that once Carol has cleared her debts and her obligations to others, she can consider travel and that she will probably go somewhere new to her, or she might do something different from her usual holiday.

18: Journalling

Here is a journal page idea for you to try.

JOURNAL NOTES

Name of questioner: ………..…......……………………………….……

Date of reading: ………………….....…..……………………………….

Type of spread: ……………………....…..……………………….…….

Sketch of the spread:

- The first card and your interpretation of its meaning.
- The second card and your interpretation.
- The third card and your interpretation.
- The fourth card and your interpretation.
- The fifth card and your interpretation.
- The sixth card and your interpretation.

What do you think this is telling your questioner? Is it advice that the reading seems to be giving, anything unusual or unexpected, or anything else you think is worth making a note of?

……………....………………………………………………………….

……………....………………………………………………………….

JOURNAL NOTES

Name of questioner: ………….....…………………..……………….……..

Date of reading: ……………………....…..…………………………..…….

Type of spread: ………………………....…………………………..….……

Sketch of the spread:

- The first card and your interpretation of its meaning.
- The second card and your interpretation.
- The third card and your interpretation.
- The fourth card and your interpretation.
- The fifth card and your interpretation.
- The sixth card and your interpretation.

What do you think this is telling your questioner? Is it advice that the reading seems to be giving, anything unusual or unexpected, or anything else you think is worth making a note of?

…....……………………………………………………………………….

…......…………………………………………………………………….

19: Tarot As A Profession

I have written a separate book called "Mind, Body and Spirit as a Career" about working as a reader or a therapist which goes into the subject in great depth, but this section will give you some helpful information.

Psychic Fairs
Psychic fairs are a good way of earning a little money. Doing readings for complete strangers at fairs will test your ability, while you will be among like-minded people and in a pleasant atmosphere. The work can be fun, and you could even make a small profit. You need to book a table and take a pretty cloth to put on it and whatever decks of cards that you want to use. In the past, we used to record readings and supply tapes or discs with the recording to the clients, but these days, people record readings on their mobile phones, so that is one less expense that you need to allow for. It is a good idea to take a flask of coffee and a sandwich with you, as it may be difficult to leave the stand for any length of time.

Safety
It sounds like a great idea to work from home because it is inexpensive and convenient, but you must take care about who you allow into your home. It is a good idea to work while other members of your family are somewhere nearby, as that will deter those whose intentions towards you are less than wholesome. Both men and women are vulnerable to being accused of things they haven't done, so where such things as healing and massage are concerned, it is better to work in a group situation where you will be protected. Having said this, if you know that your clients are decent people, working from home is a good option.

Clients
Most clients are lovely, well-meaning people, and it is a pleasure to read for them, but some want specialist advice that you can't give. Some clients expect us to solve convoluted legal, medical, housing or marital problems, but all you can do is be sympathetic, tell the client what the cards say and suggest they seek professional advice elsewhere.

Clients can ask things of us that we are in no position to answer. For example, I remember one client whose beloved dog had died, so she had gone out and bought a new puppy of the same breed as her previous dog, and she wanted assurance that the puppy was a reincarnation of her original pet. This wasn't something that I could do via my own skills in Tarot, astrology or palmistry, so I suggested she visit a medium and a regression therapist. Needless to say, I didn't charge her for the reading. My own opinion was that the original dog hadn't been dead long enough to reincarnate, but the poor woman was in pain and needed reassurance from the right kind of practitioner.

The Unbelievers
Some clients make you wonder why they bother to go for readings at all. These are usually women of the "battle-axe" type. They sit with their arms crossed defensively across their bosoms, with their lower jaws jutting out in a belligerent manner, clearly setting out to test the reader. Such people are oblivious to the fact that an innocuous question doesn't imply any inability to perform a perfectly good reading. If you are silly enough to ask them a question, such as, "Do you have children?" they will pounce on you, saying, "You tell me!"

If they unnerve you to the point where you can't give them a reading, don't take any money from them; usher them out and forget them. If you can manage to read for them, here is a tip you will never see in any book on Tarot, psychism or anything else of the kind. Look closely at their eyes, because every time you come up with something they know is right, their irises will contract in a kind of twitch. It doesn't matter how hard they try to keep a straight face and how hard they work at avoiding giving anything away, they can't control their irises. This can give you a magical feeling of satisfaction in this challenging situation.

Lovely Clients and Nice Readers
Fortunately, the vast majority of clients are lovely people who enjoy a reading and who get something useful from it. However, we tend to remember the difficult or awkward ones, like the obese woman who plopped herself down on one reader's sofa and broke it.

Other Products
Don't sell other products or services to your Tarot clientele. You can put leaflets on the table about these things, and if your client wants to take the leaflet, that is fair enough. If you have written a book, you can keep a copy nearby in case someone wants to look at it, but don't push it onto anybody.

19: Tarot as a Profession

Money and the Tax Man

Keep a note of the money you spend on your business and always get receipts for everything that you buy and keep them to show how you spent the money. Keep a note of the money you make as well, so when the time comes to deal with taxation, you will have the figures ready. Never try to cheat the tax man; do not claim benefits and work on the side as well. The Department for Work and Pensions (DWP) always finds out what people are doing, and there can be unpleasant consequences. If your affairs are complicated, use the services of an accountant to help you sort things out and to keep you on the right side of the law. It will be money well spent, and what you pay the accountant is a legitimate expense that you put against tax.

Insurance

You need to insure the contents of your home, and you need Public Liability insurance and Professional Indemnity insurance.

Many things can arise that could go wrong when dealing with people in general, and two things are essential if you do readings for payment.

First of all, have a prominent notice (perhaps a leaflet to give to your clients), providing general information about you and your business, but adding a clear disclaimer that the reading is given for entertainment purposes only, is not claimed to be comprehensive, that you decline any responsibility for actual or alleged damages arising from the reading and that if the client is dissatisfied with the reading, they are only entitled to a refund of the money paid for the reading. If the client won't accept these conditions, then you should not read for them.

20: Your First Fee Paying Client

Your first fee-paying client is likely to be a friend of a friend, and we will assume they will come to your home. Your client is likely to be a woman, and she may come on her own, but the chances are she will bring a friend along. In my days of doing readings, I was always happy for friends to sit in on the reading, but I always asked the client if that was what she wanted, as not all of them do. You will now have to find somewhere for the friend to wait, which could be a chair in your hallway or your kitchen. Make sure you have somewhere quiet for the reading without being interrupted by children or pets, and leave your phone in another room for the time being.

You can have some New Age music playing. You can light a candle or burn some incense if you like, but turn the music off before you start the actual reading because it will distract both you and your client. Not everyone likes incense, and it makes some people cough, so a diffuser might be a better idea, but ensure that diffusers, candles and so on aren't likely to start a fire.

I prefer not to play any kind of music or to use any "props", but each person should do what they think is best.

Sit your client down nearby and give her the cards to shuffle. Don't chat with her because you now need to create a quiet, meditative atmosphere. Let her shuffle for as long as she likes, and then ask her to put the cards down on the table. I like to ask my clients to break the cards into three piles and to choose one pile for the reading, but you must do whatever feels right for you. While all this is going on, ask the universe to help you give a successful and helpful reading and do your best to relax.

20: Your First Fee-Paying Client

Balance
Lay the cards out in a generalised spread of your choice and see what the balance looks like. The following will show you what I mean by this.

There are roughly two-thirds of Minor Arcana cards to Major Arcana in a Tarot deck, so a truly balanced reading should have a two-thirds / one-third combination. Therefore, a lot of Major Arcana cards in the spread suggest that your client is going through some form of turmoil at the time of the reading. She may be making important decisions at this time, or she may be in the hands of fate rather than being able to control her own destiny.

Suppose there are very few Major Arcana cards on display. In that case, her life is relatively smooth, and she doesn't have to cope with significant disturbances to her usual routine. She may still have worries, but her world is not being turned upside down at this time.

If the spread has a number of Court cards, there are several people in the client's environment. Sometimes, a number of cards show that the client works with a group of people, or maybe her pastimes, charitable work or socialising bring her into contact with a number of people. While this is nice for her, these people aren't a significant factor in her life. A couple of court cards are a more meaningful indicator, and it is worth taking time to consider what role the people represented by these cards may soon play in her life.

A number of Cup cards indicate an emotional situation, which may have something to do with the client's love life or perhaps some other part of her life altogether. I have seen many Cup cards in the readings of people who are putting a lot of energy and worry into a business matter or who are upset over the way money is being spent in their family circle and so on. It is a matter of working out what is causing the client anxiety.

Wand cards usually relate to day-to-day matters, work, people, creative ventures and life in general, and it isn't unusual to see plenty of these. They can have a connection to learning and discovery, travel, lots of conversation and communication. There may be house moves or the start of some enterprise when lots of Wands turn up in a reading.

Pentacles refer to finances, resources, valuable matters, business and security, so these issues come to the fore if there are plenty of these in the reading. However, they can refer to property and land.

Swords can be challenging to analyse. Firstly, they can show troubles and illness, even operations and serious matters of that kind. Secondly, Swords can also mean getting to grips with difficulties and dealing with them, even to the point of doing things that don't suit those around the client. In occasional cases, Swords relate to metal and such things as getting vehicles fixed, engineering of various kinds, working with tools, even as a doctor or a nurse and being around implements.

Once you have a feel for the spread, allow your instinct to guide you. If you feel that what you are seeing is right – or you think that it reflects what will happen in the client's life in the future – tell the client what you are "getting".

After the reading is finished, the client will usually be happy to tell you what is going on in her life and whether the cards were accurate or not; this feedback will be very helpful to you. However, if your client just wants to go away and contemplate the reading on her own, that is her right. As long as you feel you have done a good job and she seems happy with your work, take your fee and thank your guides, angels, the universe and your higher consciousness for the help they have all given you. Blow out candles and diffusers and make yourself a nice cup of coffee to settle your nerves. Your next reading will be less stressful, and soon, you will feel as though you have been giving readings all your life, and the more you do, the more your psychic and intuitive abilities will develop.

Conclusion

Over many years, astrology and the Tarot have helped my husband and me to cope with some very tough times, and they have given us hope when we most needed it. I hope this book shows you how to get the best from the Tarot for yourself, your loved ones and your clients. Trust the cards to tell you the truth and use them with the best of intentions to help and heal those who need their guidance. Don't forget to enjoy being a Tarot reader, though, as well as being a wise guide to those who seek your help!

I wish you the very best of luck!

Index

A
Alliette, Jean-Baptiste 6
Alternative Meanings 21
Alternative names for the suits 14
Angela 142
Aquarius 61
Archetypes 13
Aries 35
Aries, Leo and Sagittarius 73
Astrological Spread 149
astrology 7
athame 199

B
Basic Spread of Seven Cards 136
Bingham, Dave 195
Bingham, Eve 17, 195
Boiardo-Viti Tarocchi 6
British Astrological and Psychic Society 17, 195
Bronson, Charles 189
Buddhism 7

C
Cancer 41
Capricorn 57
Carina 7
Celtic Cross 148
China 6
Choose-it-Yourself Spread 137
clairvoyant 16
Clearing the Chakras 17
Closing the Chakras 16
Colman-Smith, Pamela 7
Colour 19, 162
Colour Oddments 169

Colours and Astrology 167
Consequences Spread 142
Court Cards 13, 71
Crowley, Aleister 6
Cups, Four of 12
Curtis, Fred 195

D
Days, Weeks and Months 22
decanates 184
Decans and the Tarot 188
Decans, The 186
Designated Spread 136
Devil card 13
Direction on the Cards 22

E
element of Air 27
Element of Air 198
Element of Earth 198
Element of Fire 198
Element of Spirit 199
Element of Water 199
Elements 198
Ellen, Barbara 16
Energising a New Deck 9
Etteilla 6

F
Fate 7
Fire 67, 73
Fire signs 73
Ford, Harrison 189
Four-Card Exercise 157
Free Will 7

Index

G
Gemini 39
Gemini, Libra and Aquarius 121
Genesis 26
Golden Dawn 6

H
Harris, Lady Frieda 7
Health Reading 21
Hindle, Renée 195
Hippocratic Oath 9

I
If All Else Fails 157

J
Jean Noblet cards 6
Jenny's Story 152
Journals 24
Judgement 66
Jupiter 47
Justice 48

K
Kabbalah 6, 7, 15
Kay 4
Keith 194
Key Ideas 19

L
Large Spreads 152
Leo 43
Letter: Aleph 27
Letter: Ayin 57
Letter: Beth 29
Letter: Cheth 41
Letter: Daleth 33
Letter: Gimal 31
Letter: Hey 35
Letter: Keph 47
Letter: Lamed 49

Letter: Mem 51
Letter: Nun 53
Letter: Peh 59
Letter: Qof 63
Letter: Resh 65
Letter: Samekh 55
Letter: Shin 67
Letter: Tav 69
Letter: Teth 43
Letter: Tzaddi 61
Letter: Vau 37
Letter: Yod 45
Letter: Zain 39
Libra 49
Linda 153
Linking Dissimilar Cards 156
Linking Similar Cards 155
Linking Two Cards 155
Luke 138
Lumley, Joanna 189

M
Major Arcana 14
Mamluk deck 6
Mars 59
Marseille Tarot 6
meditation 7, 17
medium 16
Mercury 29
Mike 191, 194
Mike's Business 191
Minchiati 6
Minor Arcana 14
Moon 31
Moon, Days and Time 200

N
Neptune 51
New Age 7
Numbers, Brief Description of 181
Numerology and the Tarot 180

The Tarot Journey in Colour

O
occult 7
Odin 50
Oracle cards 10

P
Past, Present and Future 141
Picking up Clues 20
Pisces 63
Playing cards 10
Pluto 67
Psychic Fairs 207
Psychic Training 16
Pyramid, The 147

R
Reading by Images Alone 18
Relationships on the Cards 137
Reversed Cards 11
Rider Waite deck 5, 6
Rodney 8
Runes 50
Russell, Myra 195

S
Sagittarius 55
Saturn 69
Scientific Method 185
Scorpio 53
seasons 71
Sforza, Francesco 6
significator 11
skin ailment 13
Smith, Gordon 195
Sola-Busca 6
Spellcasting 15
Strength 42
Suits 71
Sun 65
Swiss Tarot 4
Swords, Queen of 12

T
Tarocco Bolognese 6
Tarot journal 21
Taurus 37
Taurus, Virgo and Capricorn 105
Temperance 54
The Chariot 40
The Devil 56
The Emperor 34
The Empress 32
The Fool 26
The Fool's Journey 25
The Hanged Man 50
The Hermit 44
The Hierophant 36
The High Priestess 30
The Magician 28
The Moon 62
The Star 60
The Sun 64
The Tower 58
The Wheel of Fortune 46
The World 68
Thoth deck 6
Tibetan monks 6
Timing On the Cards 22
Tina 145
Towers, Jackie 23
Tree of Life Spread 152
Trionfi 6
Twelve-Month Method 22
Two Roads 137

U
Unbelievers 208
Uranus 27

V
Venus 33
Very Unusual Reading 194
Virgo 45

Index

Visconti-Sforza Tarot 6
Visconti, Filippo Maria 6

W
Waite, Arthur Edward 6
Wicca 15
Working Backwards 24

Y
Yang 13
Yin 13

www.ingramcontent.com/pod-product-compliance
Lightning Source LLC
Chambersburg PA
CBHW041439300426
44114CB00026B/2942